FRESH mexico

FRESH mexico

100 SIMPLE RECIPES FOR TRUE MEXICAN FLAVOR

MARCELA VALLADOLID

PHOTOGRAPHS BY AMY KALYN SIMS

CLARKSON POTTER | PUBLISHERS | NEW YORK

Published in the United States by Clarkson Potter/Publishers, an imprint of
the Crown Publishing Group, a division of Random House, Inc., New York.
www.crownpublishing.com
www.clarksonpotter.com

CLARKSON POTTER is a trademark and POTTER with colophon is a
registered trademark of Random House, Inc.

Library of Congress Cataloging-in-Publication Data
Valladolid, Marcela.
Fresh Mexico / Marcela Valladolid. — 1st ed.
Includes index.
1. Cookery, Mexican.   2. Cookery, Mexico.   I. Title.
TX716.M4V32   2009
641.5972—dc22   2008051293

ISBN 978-0-307-45110-1

Printed in China

Design by Amy Sly

10 9 8 7 6 5 4 3 2 1

First Edition

PARA MI MAMÁ

CONTENTS

INTRODUCTION

During an interview I did once with a certain Baja magazine, editor-in-chief Ada Oliver and I discussed the state of Mexican food in my home country and around the world. I was excited to meet Ada, but I never expected that with one remark she would help me define the course of my culinary career. She had only one request of me (if I ever hit the big time). "Please," she said, "tell North America that there is no yellow cheese in Mexico!"

It clicked. I thought of all the misdirected interpretations of my beloved home country's cuisine: Cheddar cheese–stuffed quesadillas, tortilla chips drowning in neon yellow "cheez" (a.k.a. nachos), and the ubiquitous everything-but-the-kitchen-sink burritos that show up in Mexican restaurants masquerading as the real deal across the United States.

Where were the authentic, easy-to-prepare Mexican recipes that I grew up with? Where were the ceviches made with the freshest seafood? Why wasn't anyone high-lighting the exciting evolution of Mexican cuisine, as seen in dishes like Cuitlacoche Crêpes with Poblano Chile Cream (page 37)? Churros are lovely but what about Mango Pockets with Cinnamon Cream (page 199) or the Pastel de Tres Leches (page 209), which take *canela* (cinnamon) to a whole new level?

Mexican cuisine is full of brilliant fresh flavors, and I'm desperate to share them with you. In these pages, you will find recipes that represent modern Mexico, traditional Mexico, and me. They are accessible—made with ingredients you can find easily—yet very representative of Mexican food today.

Back to the yellow cheese. As Ada said, you won't find any in Mexico! The closest is Chihuahua cheese, also known as Menonita, after the Mennonite communities who first produced it in northern Mexico. Unlike most Mexican cheeses, which are white, Chihuahua is pale yellow and varies from mild to sharp, just like Cheddar. But let me be clear—it's not Cheddar, nor is it bright yellow. Don't get me wrong—I love Cheddar cheese, and chimichangas, and margaritas (which we don't actually drink all that much south of the border). But if you think that's all there is to Mexican food, you're missing out on so much.

It's my nature to break stereotypes, and I'm in a good position to do it. I'm a Tijuana native. Yes, Tijuana, which is actually pronounced Tee-who-ON-na, not Tia-wanna. I've been crossing the San Ysidro international border, between Tijuana and San Diego, my entire life. Trust me, I've heard more than my share of jokes at the expense of my beloved hometown.

But how is this relevant to these recipes? Simple. Growing up in a border town, I was influenced by both Mexican and American cultures. When *El Chavo del Ocho* went to commercial break, I would flip through the channels and invariably land on a U.S. channel advertising "crunchy Mexican beef tacos." I cringed every time. A crunchy beef taco may taste good, but it is not Mexican! And you probably won't find one in a reputable Mexican cookbook.

I grew up with the real stuff: crickets, ant roe, and corn fungus—and love it I did. Now that's not what this book is about either, but I firmly believe that you're allowed to bend or break the rules only after you understand and respect them. And I know the rules. Complex mole was a standard weeknight dinner in my childhood home, spicy enchiladas often showed up for breakfast, and homemade salsas, sweet hibiscus tea, and tortillas were all staples.

So while the crickets were chilling in my pantry, I discovered early on that I also loved shopping (and the ingredients) at the markets in San Diego. I'm the first one to admit life is much more practical on the northern side of the border. You can find anything you want if you look hard enough. Who needs to make puff pastry or fresh pasta when you can find perfect, ready-made dough in the frozen foods section of your supermarket? So why not marry the two? Why not keep it Mexican at its roots but easy to prepare?

My food, as you will find in this book, is very much like me. It's Mexican but influenced by other cultures. It is sophisticated in its presentation but easy to prepare. My recipes are also not the 100 percent authentic and traditional moles, pipiáns, or salsas you'll find in cookbooks by masters like Diana Kennedy. The books written by Miss Kennedy in the 1970s were passed down to me from my grandfather and have

BUÑUELOS

been instrumental in my formation as a professional cook. But I don't have time for that kind of cooking when I have to get dinner on the table for my young son.

Here you get all of the authentic flavors without the fuss. No shopping for fifteen hard-to-find ingredients and then slaving in the kitchen for hours. The vast majority of the ingredients here are readily available in U.S. supermarkets. Of course I hope a few of these dishes might inspire you to visit your local Latin market, but if you don't have one, or don't have the time, I give suitable substitutes for almost every specialty ingredient that will yield equally authentic—but most important, delicious—results.

I've even added an "＊" to denote the recipes that are low in fat and a "🕐" to indicate those that can be prepared in close to 30 minutes. Let's face it: you're running out of excuses not to cook this stuff.

But first let me tell you how this all started for me personally. My passion for food and entertaining was ignited during one of my first jobs in the culinary world. I was an assistant instructor at my aunt Marcela Rodriguez's cooking school, one of the first in Tijuana. Hoping to get into a professional kitchen, I packed my '98 Mustang and landed a job as a hostess in a trendy Los Angeles restaurant. I wasn't allowed anywhere near a stovetop. For that reason, in addition to the fact that young women don't leave Tijuana unless they're in school or married—at least not in my family—I opted to enroll at the Los Angeles Culinary Institute, much to my parents' relief.

After graduation, I serendipitously landed at *Bon Appétit* magazine. A lot of what I know, I learned there. I became a much more disciplined cook as well as a student of countless cuisines and ingredients. I began to appreciate sharing delicious food with people. When *Bon Appétit* devoted an entire issue to Mexico, I spent weeks testing authentic Mexican recipes. Current editor-in-chief Barbara Fairchild, along with the other editors, described the food as exquisite. I was hooked. Opening people's eyes to the delicacies of Mexico is my calling. But I wasn't ready to spread the word quite then. As a professional cook, I knew I needed to learn pastries.

I've never enjoyed baking. I don't crave sweets and chocolate isn't my thing. (Do I hear a collective gasp?) So, I left *Bon Appétit* to specialize in classic French pastries at the Ritz-Escoffier school in Paris. I made puff pastry every day for three months. Let me tell you that I now purchase mine frozen, but if I'm put to the test, I can make the flakiest puff pastry you've ever tasted.

My experience in Paris and Tijuana taught me that I love learning and teaching. I had experience doing cooking segments on local television in Tijuana, so I moved back home with the hope of starting my own cooking school. I turned my dining room into a cooking classroom, was the food editor for a Tijuana newspaper, and appeared regularly on a morning news program.

It took Martha Stewart to slow me down. I was cast on *The Apprentice: Martha Stewart,* which led to my own cooking show, *Relatos con Sabor,* on Discovery en Español. My show takes viewers into the homes of Latinos who are keeping their traditions alive through food despite living in a foreign country. And now, here I am, grateful to have been given the opportunity to propose a new way of cooking and serving Mexican food.

As my three-year-old, Fausto, sleeps and dreams beside me this evening, I have a dream of my own:

It's a festive evening and Jane Smith from Columbia, Missouri, has invited several friends over for a Mexican dinner. She set a beautiful table with *talavera* plates and dark red Aurora's Kiss dahlias in a giant copper vase. The menu is as follows:

Chilled Avocado Soup with Scallops
Rack of Lamb with Ancho Crust
Sage and Sweet Potato Mash
Roasted Cabbage with Oregano and Oaxaca Cheese
Apricot Tequila Ice Cream topped with Pomegranate Pine Nut Brittle

Nowhere to be seen: chips drowning in bright yellow cheese.

APPETIZERS & SMALL BITES

A DIFFERENT KIND OF BURRITO

We all know and love the burrito offered in our favorite Tex-Mex joints in the U.S. You know the one I'm talking about: the bulging flour tortilla stuffed with rice, beans, grilled chicken, guacamole, sour cream, shredded cheese, and salsa. But I grew up with a different kind of burrito, a slimmer (and healthier) version, stuffed with shredded beef and served with a side of pickled jalapeños or Chiles Toreados (page 179)— a simple dish that often showed up on the dinner table to appease our appetites before the main course was served.

On my last trip to Mexico City to visit my congressman-of-a-brother, Antonio, we went to MP Café & Bistro, a wonderful restaurant in his neighborhood, Polanco. I was traveling with my mom and we had both heard wonderful things about the chef/owner, Monica Patino, and her duck burrito appetizer, so we ordered them. The rumors were true. The duck burritos, served with a tomatillo salsa, were absolutely delicious. The presentation of the dish was superb: a timbale of shredded duck meat, a small plate with the tomatillo salsa, and four mini flour tortillas served in a mini bamboo steamer. My mom was in love.

We went to that place for dinner every night we were in Mexico City. Not only were we hooked on the duck burritos, we were enamored of the restaurant's ability to provide our favorite combinations of flavors and ingredients, presented in a manner that rivaled that of the best restaurants around the world, in a chic but comfortable environment. To paint a better picture, consider that I drank a berry martini with my burritos instead of a Corona. In short, we liked dressing up for the burrito! That is what I'm offering you here.

You don't need to put on heels or a tie to prepare and serve the Baja-Mediterranean Ahi Tuna (page 23), but you can absolutely consider any one of these appetizers for a special evening with your friends. They are easy to prepare and offer a twist on the dishes your guests know and love. As beloved as our taco stands are and always will be, it's nice to have a more sophisticated alternative for authentic Mexican food.

The recipes in this chapter (and in the whole book, as you can see) are a lot like the duck burrito we discovered in the capital city (and like me, for that matter): petite and delectable, with a modern twist but traditional at the core, packed with Mexican flavor and color, and perfectly compatible with the most sophisticated menu.

THE DUCK BURRITO

ROSEMARY-SKEWERED SHRIMP MARINATED IN CHIPOTLE

15 fresh rosemary sprigs

¼ cup olive oil

1½ tablespoons fresh lime juice

2 garlic cloves, minced

3 tablespoons chopped fresh cilantro

2 teaspoons ground chipotle chile

Salt and freshly ground black pepper

1 pound raw medium shrimp, peeled but tails left intact, and deveined

Lime wedges, for serving

Fresh rosemary grows rampant in my backyard, which is only part of the reason these skewers top my list of favorite appetizers. Rosemary adds smoky flavor and a decorative flourish to a simple shrimp starter. Check the USDA plant hardiness zones to see which herbs thrive in your area. Fresh herbs make a huge difference in any dish, and you'll save money by growing them at home instead of buying them. The Mediterranean rosemary pairs nicely with the smoky chipotle and fresh cilantro.

Remove the leaves from half the length of each rosemary sprig, and set the sprigs aside. Chop enough of the leaves to make 1½ teaspoons. (Reserve any remaining leaves for another use.)

Combine the olive oil, lime juice, garlic, cilantro, ground chipotle, and chopped rosemary in a medium bowl. Season the marinade with salt and black pepper to taste. Add the shrimp and toss until coated. Let stand for 5 minutes. Then skewer 2 shrimp on each rosemary sprig.

Heat a large heavy sauté pan (or *comal*) over high heat. Add the skewers and cook for 1 minute per side, or until the shrimp are cooked through. Transfer the skewers to a platter, garnish with the lime wedges, and serve immediately.

TIP USE THE SAME MARINADE ON CHICKEN BREASTS AND ON WHOLE CHICKENS FOR ROASTING. IT'S ALSO GREAT ON ANY WHITE FISH FILLET; JUST ADD A COUPLE OF TABLESPOONS OF BUTTER TO THE PAN DRIPPINGS AFTER THE FISH HAS BEEN COOKED AND REMOVED. DRIZZLE THE SAUCE OVER THE FISH AND SERVE!

TILAPIA CEVICHE

2 pounds sushi-grade tilapia, finely diced (see Tips, page 23)

15 limes: 14 halved, 1 cut into wedges

½ cup chopped seeded tomato

½ cup chopped seeded cucumber

⅓ cup finely chopped onion

¼ cup chopped fresh cilantro

Salt and freshly ground black pepper

½ cup clam-tomato juice (such as Clamato; optional)

1 tablespoon bottled hot sauce (such as Huichol; optional)

Grilled tostadas (see Tips, page 23)

Mayonnaise, for spreading

1 avocado, halved, pitted, peeled, and thinly sliced

I went to a restaurant opening in Los Angeles where they served a trio of ceviches made with parboiled seafood. *No!* Ceviche should always be made using raw ultra-fresh, or "sushi-grade," fish. In this recipe I use tilapia, but feel free to substitute whatever your local fishmonger recommends that day. The citrus marinade "cooks" the fish without heat. Traditional ceviche is left to marinate for up to 3 hours, but in this recipe you'll have fresh, delicious ceviche in 15 minutes. As my *abuelo* always said, "Don't worry, the lime kills everything."

For a more traditional ceviche, omit the clam-tomato juice and the hot sauce, which add a sour and spicy kick.

Place the tilapia in a medium bowl. Squeeze the juice from the lime halves over the fish and mix gently to combine. Chill in the refrigerator until the fish is white throughout, about 15 minutes.

Drain off the lime juice, gently squeezing the fish with your hands. Discard the lime juice. Mix the tomato, cucumber, onion, and cilantro with the fish. Season with salt and pepper to taste. Add the clam-tomato juice and the hot sauce, if desired.

Spread the tostadas generously with mayonnaise. Top the tostadas with the ceviche. Arrange the avocado slices on top of the ceviche and serve immediately, with the lime wedges alongside.

BAJA-MEDITERRANEAN AHI TUNA

1 tablespoon olive oil

3 tablespoons soy sauce

2 tablespoons fresh lime juice

1 tablespoon fresh orange juice

1½ pounds sushi-grade ahi tuna, diced (see Tips)

¼ cup diced peeled seeded cucumber

2 tablespoons capers, drained

2 tablespoons sesame seeds, toasted (see Tips)

¼ cup sliced pitted kalamata olives

Salt and freshly ground black pepper

Fresh cilantro, for serving, optional

Grilled tostadas (see Tips), for serving

This is a simple, refreshing dish that perfectly represents the current trend in Baja-Mediterranean cuisine: the fusion of local ingredients and cooking techniques with European (mostly Mediterranean) ingredients, with an occasional Asian ingredient showing up in the mix. Variations of this dish pop up in restaurants all around Mexico, some adding spicy avocado dressing or fresh orange juice to the mix. I like to keep it simple to let the fresh taste of the ingredients shine through.

Mix the olive oil, soy sauce, lime juice, and orange juice in a small bowl. Set the vinaigrette aside.

Carefully mix the diced tuna, cucumber, capers, toasted sesame seeds, and olives together in a large bowl. Add the vinaigrette and toss gently to combine. Season with salt and pepper to taste.

Divide the ceviche among chilled bowls, sprinkle with cilantro, if desired, and serve with grilled tostadas.

TIPS SEAFOOD IS EASIEST TO DICE WHEN IT IS PARTIALLY FROZEN; THIS ALSO MAKES FOR A MUCH CLEANER PRESENTATION. USE A VERY SHARP KNIFE.

TO TOAST THE SESAME SEEDS, ADD THEM TO A SMALL SKILLET SET OVER MEDIUM-LOW HEAT AND COOK, STIRRING FREQUENTLY, UNTIL TOASTED AND FRAGRANT, ABOUT 3 MINUTES.

AS FOR THE GRILLED TOSTADAS, JUST THROW A COUPLE OF CORN TORTILLAS ON AN OUTDOOR GRILL, OR ON A GRILL PAN, AND LET THEM DRY OUT OVER MEDIUM HEAT UNTIL THEY ARE NICE AND CRUNCHY. TEAR THEM INTO LARGE PIECES TO SERVE.

DEVILED EGGS WITH ANCHO, SOUR CREAM, AND CILANTRO

10 large hard-boiled eggs, peeled and halved lengthwise (see opposite)

1 ancho chile, stemmed and seeded

⅓ cup sour cream

3 tablespoons mayonnaise (or Homemade Chipotle Mayo, page 187)

2 tablespoons chopped fresh cilantro

1 teaspoon Dijon mustard

1 teaspoon fresh lemon juice

½ teaspoon salt

½ teaspoon freshly ground black pepper

Deviled eggs might not be the first thing you think of when planning an appetizer menu. But when sprinkled with smoky ancho chile and bright cilantro, these retro bites are always the most talked-about dish at any gathering at my house. I use a spice grinder to pulverize the dried chile, but you can find already ground ancho chile in many supermarkets and in Latin markets; you'll need 1 teaspoon.

Carefully scoop the yolks from the egg halves, dropping them into a large bowl. Arrange the empty egg halves on a large platter.

Tear the chile into small pieces and place it in a spice grinder. Grind to a powder. Add 1 teaspoon of this ground chile to the egg yolks. Add the sour cream, mayonnaise, cilantro, mustard, lemon juice, salt, and pepper, and mash with a fork until smooth.

Spoon the filling into each of the egg halves, mounding it slightly. (The deviled eggs can be prepared 2 hours ahead. Cover and refrigerate.) Serve with 1 teaspoon of the remaining chile powder sifted over the eggs, if desired.

HARD-BOILED EGGS

How to cook the perfect hard-boiled egg? Start off with week-old eggs because fresh eggs are harder to peel. Place the eggs (as many as you want) in a saucepan and add enough cold water to cover by 1 inch. Bring to a boil over medium-high heat. When the water comes to a rapid boil, cook for exactly 8 minutes. Then remove the pan from the heat and let the eggs cool in the water. Once they are cool, peel under cold running water.

SPICY CRAB CAKES TOPPED WITH GUACAMOLE

Nonstick cooking spray

1 pound lump crabmeat, picked over to remove any shell and cartilage

2 tablespoons mayonnaise (or Homemade Chipotle Mayo, page 187)

¼ cup chopped scallions (white and pale green parts only)

1 tablespoon plus 1 teaspoon fresh lime juice

½ cup plus 2 tablespoons chopped fresh cilantro

½ teaspoon habanero hot sauce

Salt and freshly ground black pepper

1 cup panko bread crumbs (Japanese bread crumbs)

2 firm but ripe avocados, halved, pitted, and peeled

2 tablespoons minced onion

Crab cakes get a festive kick when coated in crunchy panko bread crumbs mixed with cilantro and then topped with a simple guacamole. This is the guacamole that was made on a regular basis at my house when I was growing up. I don't like fussy guacamoles that mask the fresh flavor of a perfectly ripe avocado.
This crab cake mixture is eggless and is baked rather than fried, yielding a lighter dish with more crab flavor.

Preheat the oven to 400°F.

Spray a baking sheet with nonstick cooking spray.

Mix the crabmeat, mayonnaise, scallions, 1 tablespoon of the lime juice, ¼ cup of the cilantro, and the hot sauce together in a small bowl. Season to taste with salt and pepper.

Mix the panko bread crumbs and ¼ cup of the remaining cilantro on a plate. Divide the crab mixture into 8 equal mounds. Form 1 mound into a ¾-inch-thick patty, and then carefully turn the patty in the crumb mixture to coat it on both sides. Transfer it to the prepared baking sheet. Repeat with the remaining 7 mounds. Bake the crab cakes for 10 minutes, or until heated through.

Meanwhile, coarsely mash the avocados in a medium bowl. Lightly mix in the onion, remaining 2 tablespoons cilantro, and remaining 1 teaspoon lime juice. Season the guacamole liberally with salt and pepper.

Transfer the crab cakes to a serving platter, top each one with a tablespoon of guacamole, and serve.

SMOKED MARLIN QUESADILLAS

1 tablespoon olive oil

1 pound smoked marlin, shredded

1 green bell pepper, stemmed, seeded, and diced

1 small white onion, minced

2 tomatoes, chopped

1 cup canned tomato puree

1 teaspoon dried oregano

1 bay leaf

Hungarian sweet paprika, to taste

Salt and freshly ground black pepper

Ten 6-inch corn tortillas

1½ cups shredded Oaxaca cheese or mozzarella cheese

Lime wedges, for serving

Bottled hot sauce, for serving

This is my version of the famous Baja *taco gobernador,* which is a shrimp-stuffed quesadilla. The marlin adds a distinctive smoked flavor that makes this a very special kind of quesadilla. If you must substitute, you can use canned tuna—just make sure it is well drained, and cook the filling an additional 4 minutes to allow the moisture from the tuna to evaporate.

Heat the olive oil in a large heavy saucepan over medium-high heat. Add the marlin, bell pepper, onion, tomatoes, tomato puree, oregano, and bay leaf. Cook to combine the flavors, about 8 minutes. Season to taste with paprika, salt, and pepper. Remove from the heat.

Heat a large heavy skillet over medium-high heat. Add 2 corn tortillas, side by side, to heat. Place a small mound of cheese on one side of each tortilla. Wait until the cheese melts slightly, about 1 minute, and then add about 2 tablespoons of the marlin mixture to each tortilla (discard the bay leaf). Fold the tortillas over into half-moons and cook to melt the cheese completely, another minute or two. Transfer the quesadillas to a platter and keep warm.

Repeat with the remaining tortillas, cheese, and marlin mixture. Serve with lime wedges and hot sauce on the side.

SALSA MAGGI

Maggi seasoning sauce is a staple in Mexican cooking. There are folks in Mexico who swear we came up with the concoction, but all credit has to be given to the Swiss. The Maggi company became hugely popular in the early 1900s for producing the bouillon cube. Maggi seasoning sauce, or Salsa Maggi, was first intended to be used as a cheap substitute for meat extract, but it is now a staple seasoning in all of Latin America, some of Europe, and Asia. Use it sparingly, as it is packed with flavor. It is similar to soy sauce but contains no soy. I like to use it to flavor ceviches, chicken salads, and soups, or to just squirt a couple of dashes over my scrambled eggs. You can find it in some supermarkets and in most Latin markets.

PEDRO'S OYSTERS ON THE HALF SHELL

12 fresh oysters, shucked and resting in their bottom shell

¾ cup minced white onion

½ cup chopped fresh cilantro

¼ cup fresh lime juice

3 tablespoons clam-tomato juice (such as Clamato; optional)

4 teaspoons Maggi seasoning sauce (see opposite)

2 tablespoons Worcestershire sauce

1 teaspoon minced seeded serrano chile

1 teaspoon bottled hot sauce (such as Huichol)

Salt

For many years a professional cook who specialized in seafood dishes prepared the meals at my parents' house. Pedro Rocha would go to the fish market with my dad, bring home whatever had been caught that day, and turn it into an incredible meal for the family or for my father's friends (who often came just for the food). Many of my seafood dishes are inspired by or derived from dishes Pedro taught me to make. This is one of them, and it's always a favorite with my friends. As soon as we figure out how to get Pedro a passport, we're opening a fish restaurant in the United States!

Arrange the oysters, preferably over crushed ice, on a platter.

Mix the onion, cilantro, lime juice, clam-tomato juice if using, Maggi sauce, Worcestershire sauce, serrano chile, and hot sauce in a medium bowl. Season the salsa to taste with a little salt. Spoon about 1 tablespoon of the salsa over each oyster, and serve immediately.

TIJUANA-STYLE SUSHI ROLL

¾ cup whole milk

2 large eggs

1 large egg yolk

2 cups (loosely packed) fresh spinach

1 cup (loosely packed) fresh cilantro

½ cup all-purpose flour

3 tablespoons unsalted butter, melted

1 serrano chile, stemmed and seeded

Salt

2 mangoes, peeled and pitted

2 tablespoons mayonnaise

1 tablespoon sugar

1 teaspoon soy sauce

½ teaspoon dry mustard

¼ teaspoon wasabi paste

Freshly ground black pepper

Nonstick cooking spray

8 ounces lump crabmeat, picked over to remove any shell and cartilage

I had to include Baja sushi because I think the fusion of Asian techniques and Mexican ingredients is phenomenal! This recipe, which uses a spinach crêpe as a wrapper instead of nori (seaweed), comes from my friend Andres Brambila, who owns Negai, a wonderful sushi restaurant in Tijuana.

Combine the milk, eggs, and egg yolk in a blender and blend to combine. Add the spinach, cilantro, flour, butter, serrano chile, and ½ teaspoon salt, and blend until very smooth. Transfer the crêpe batter to a medium bowl. Let the batter stand for 30 minutes.

In a clean blender, blend the mangoes with the mayonnaise, sugar, soy sauce, dry mustard, and wasabi paste until smooth. Season the mango sauce to taste with salt and black pepper.

Heat a crêpe pan, or a nonstick skillet measuring 6 to 7 inches across the bottom, over moderate heat until it is hot. Spray the pan lightly with nonstick cooking spray, and heat it until it is hot but not smoking. Add a scant ¼ cup of the crêpe batter to the pan. Immediately tilt and rotate the pan quickly to cover the bottom with a layer of batter. Cook the crêpe for 1 minute, or until the top appears almost dry. Loosen the edge of the crêpe with a spatula, turn the crêpe over, and cook the other side lightly. Transfer the crêpe to a plate. Make more crêpes with the remaining batter in the same manner, spraying the pan lightly with nonstick cooking spray as necessary and stacking them

RECIPE CONTINUES

1 teaspoon hot chile sauce (such as sriracha)

1 teaspoon masago caviar

8 medium cooked shrimp, peeled and halved lengthwise

1 avocado, halved, pitted, peeled, and thinly sliced

one on top of the other on the plate. (The crêpes can be made 3 days in advance, wrapped in plastic wrap, and chilled.)

Mix the crabmeat, hot chile sauce, and masago in a small bowl.

Place 1 crêpe on a work surface and spoon 2 to 3 table-spoons of the crab mixture down the center of the crêpe. Top with 2 shrimp halves and 2 or 3 avocado slices. Roll up the crêpe into a cylinder. Cut it into 4 equal pieces, as you would a sushi roll. Spread 1 tablespoon of the mango sauce on a plate. Place the sliced roll on top of the sauce. Repeat with the remaining crêpes, filling, and sauce.

JALAPEÑO AND CHEESE STUFFED OLIVES

One 21-ounce jar large jalapeño-stuffed olives

2 ounces Monterey Jack cheese, cut into matchstick-size strips

1 cup fresh bread crumbs

2 large eggs

½ cup all-purpose flour

Olive oil, for panfrying

I was visiting my father one afternoon when unexpected guests stopped by for a game of *futbol.* He turned to me and said, "Quick, make me an appetizer, chef!" There was *nothing* remotely exciting in the fridge and the pantry appeared to be just as hopeless, until I noticed a jar of jalapeño-stuffed olives. Stuffed with cheese, breaded, and panfried, these little guys disappeared before anything else I made was given a second glance. They are great with an ice-cold *cerveza* and store-bought tartar sauce for dipping.

Drain the olives and rinse them under cold running water. Carefully stuff a strip of cheese alongside the jalapeño in each olive.

Put the bread crumbs in a medium bowl. Crack the eggs into another medium bowl and whisk until combined.

Place half of the flour in a fine-mesh sieve, add half of the olives, and toss to coat. Transfer the olives to the bowl with the beaten eggs, and stir gently to coat the olives all over with the egg. Transfer the olives to the bowl with the bread crumbs, and toss to coat completely. Transfer the breaded olives to a plate. Repeat with the remaining flour, olives, egg, and bread crumbs. (The olives can be breaded 1 day ahead. Cover and refrigerate.)

Place a medium saucepan over medium-high heat, and add enough olive oil to reach halfway up the sides of the pan. Heat the oil to 350°F. Working in 2 batches, fry the breaded olives for 2 minutes, or until golden brown. Transfer them to paper towels to drain. Serve immediately.

POBLANO CHILES

Poblano chiles are Mexico's most popular chile, with a peak season from summer to early fall. Depending on the crop, they can vary from mild to very spicy. Poblanos can now be found in the produce section of most supermarkets, as well as in Mexican markets. In their dry form, they are known as anchos or mulatos; these can be found whole or ground into a powder and are used to flavor sauces.

To char poblano chiles (or any other fresh chiles), simply place the chiles over a gas flame or underneath the broiler and cook until they are blackened on all sides. Enclose them in a plastic bag and let stand for 10 minutes (this will steam the peppers and make them easier to peel). Peel, stem, and seed the chiles. Once peeled, the chiles can be chopped, sliced, or stuffed.

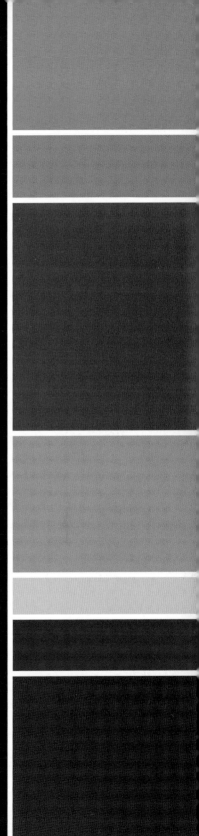

CUITLACOCHE CRÊPES WITH POBLANO CHILE CREAM

4 tablespoons (½ stick) unsalted butter, plus more for the pan

2 cups chopped onion

1 garlic clove, minced

1 to 2 serrano chiles (to taste), seeded and minced

Two 7.5-ounce cans cuitlacoche (or 2 cups sautéed wild mushrooms)

Salt and freshly ground black pepper

4 poblano chiles, charred (see page 35), stemmed, seeded, and thinly sliced

1 cup heavy cream

8 to 10 Savory Crêpes (page 39)

½ cup grated Manchego cheese

Cuitlacoche is a fungus that makes corn kernels swell to ten times their normal size, turning them an inky black color. Its smoky-sweet flavor is a cross between corn and mushroom. I grew up eating cuitlacoche stuffed in a quesadilla or in a squash blossom. It's a delicious, earthy addition to everything from quesadillas to empanadas. If you can't find canned cuitlacoche in your local Latin market, substitute sautéed wild mushrooms for an equally delicious result.

Melt 2 tablespoons of the butter in a large heavy saucepan over medium-low heat. Add 1 cup of the onion, the garlic, and the serrano chile. Sauté for 5 minutes, or until the onion is translucent. Add the cuitlacoche and stir for 5 minutes for the flavors to blend. Season to taste with salt and pepper. Set the filling aside to cool.

To make the sauce, melt the remaining 2 tablespoons butter in a medium-size heavy saucepan over medium heat. Add the remaining 1 cup onion and sauté until translucent, about 5 minutes. Add the poblano chiles and sauté for 30 seconds. Add the cream and bring to a boil. Reduce the heat and simmer for 8 minutes, or until slightly thickened. Puree the sauce in a blender until smooth. Season with salt and pepper.

RECIPE CONTINUES

Preheat the broiler. Grease a 9 x 13-inch glass baking dish with butter.

Place 1 crêpe on a cutting board. Spoon ¼ cup of the filling down the center of the crêpe. Roll it up like a burrito, enclosing the filling, and place it in the prepared baking dish. Repeat with the remaining crêpes and filling, fitting them together snugly in the dish. Pour the sauce over the crêpes. Sprinkle with the cheese. Broil until the cheese begins to brown in spots, about 10 minutes. Serve.

savory crêpes

2 large eggs

2 large egg yolks

⅔ cup whole milk

1 tablespoon plus
1 teaspoon unsalted
butter, melted

2 teaspoons sugar

¼ teaspoon salt

⅔ cup all-purpose flour

Nonstick cooking spray

Blend the eggs, egg yolks, milk, 2½ tablespoons water, the butter, sugar, and salt in a blender for 5 seconds. Add the flour in three additions, blending the batter until smooth after each addition. Cover and let rest in the blender container in the refrigerator for 1 to 2 hours. Reblend the batter for 5 seconds before using.

Heat a crêpe pan, or a nonstick skillet measuring 7 to 8 inches across the bottom, over medium-high heat until it is hot. Spray the pan lightly with nonstick cooking spray. Add a scant ¼ cup of the crêpe batter to the pan. Immediately tilt and rotate the pan quickly to cover the bottom evenly with a layer of batter. Cook the crêpe until the bottom is golden, about 30 seconds. Loosen the edges gently with a spatula, turn the crêpe over, and cook until the bottom is very lightly brown in spots, 30 to 60 seconds. Turn the crêpe out onto a plate. Repeat, using the remaining batter in the same manner, spraying the pan lightly with nonstick cooking spray as necessary and stacking the crêpes one on top of the other on the plate. (The crêpes can be made 2 days ahead. Wrap them well in plastic wrap and refrigerate.)

AVOCADO EGG ROLLS WITH CALIFORNIA CHILE–PRUNE SAUCE

3 avocados, halved, pitted, peeled, and diced

1 red bell pepper, stemmed, seeded, and finely chopped

1 tablespoon olive oil

Salt and freshly ground black pepper

Twelve 7-inch square wonton wrappers

California Chile–Prune Sauce (opposite)

1 large egg, lightly beaten

Vegetable oil, for frying

To create these vegetarian egg rolls I use wonton wrappers, which can be found in the refrigerated section in well-stocked supermarkets. You can use store-bought prune sauce in place of the California Chile–Prune Sauce; just mix some ground California chiles into the prune sauce. Either purchased or homemade, spicy prune sauce is the perfect counterpoint for fresh avocados.

Gently mix the avocados, bell pepper, and olive oil in a medium bowl. Season the avocado mixture with salt and pepper.

Place 1 wonton wrapper on a work surface. Spread 1 tablespoon of the chile-prune sauce down the center. Spoon a scant ¼ cup of the avocado mixture over the sauce. Fold the bottom of the wonton wrapper over the filling, then fold the sides of the wrapper in over the filling. Brush the top edge of the wrapper with some of the beaten egg. Roll it up tightly, pressing to seal the edge. Repeat with the remaining wonton wrappers, avocado mixture, and chile-prune sauce. (The egg rolls can be prepared 2 hours ahead. Cover and refrigerate.)

Place a medium-size heavy saucepan over medium-high heat, and add enough oil to reach halfway up the sides of the pan. Heat the oil to 350°F. Working in batches, fry the egg rolls in the hot oil, turning them occasionally, for 2 minutes, or until golden brown. Transfer the egg rolls to paper towels to drain. Serve hot or warm.

california chile—prune sauce

¾ cup honey

½ cup chopped pitted dried prunes

½ cup fresh orange juice

¼ cup fresh lime juice

4 California chiles, stemmed, seeded, and torn into pieces

Salt and freshly ground black pepper

Combine the honey, prunes, half of the orange juice, half of the lime juice, and the chiles in a small heavy saucepan. Bring to a boil over medium-high heat. Reduce the heat and simmer for 15 minutes, or until the chiles are soft. Let the sauce cool slightly.

Transfer the sauce to a blender and puree until smooth. Stir in the remaining orange and lime juices. Season to taste with salt and pepper. (The sauce can be made 2 days ahead. Cool, then cover and keep refrigerated.)

AVOCADO MOUSSE

4 ripe but firm avocados, halved, pitted, and peeled

2 tablespoons fresh lime juice

1½ teaspoons salt

¼ cup whole milk

1½ teaspoons unflavored gelatin

¼ cup diced scallions (white and pale green parts only)

2 teaspoons minced seeded jalapeño chile

½ cup heavy cream

Garlic-Oregano Crostini (recipe follows)

There are several varieties of avocado, each with a slightly different flavor. For this recipe, I use Hass, the most common type sold in supermarkets in the U.S. Choose ripe avocados (slightly firm but yielding to gentle pressure), and be sure to remove any brown spots before you start.

If you don't have time to prepare the garlic-oregano crostini, this creamy and luxurious spread is great on any savory cracker.

Line an 8½ x 4½-inch loaf pan with plastic wrap.

Combine 3 of the avocados, the lime juice, and 1 teaspoon of the salt in a food processor. Puree until smooth.

Pour the milk into a small saucepan and sprinkle the gelatin over it. Turn the heat on to low and stir for 2 minutes to dissolve the gelatin. Add this to the avocado mixture in the food processor and process to combine. Transfer the avocado mixture to a medium bowl.

Dice enough of the remaining avocado to make ½ cup. Gently mix the diced avocado, scallions, jalapeño, and remaining ½ teaspoon salt in a small bowl. Stir this into the avocado mixture.

Using an electric mixer, whip the cream until stiff peaks form. Gently fold the whipped cream into the avocado mixture. Transfer the mousse to the prepared pan. Cover with plastic wrap and chill for at least 2 hours, until set, or for up to 1 day.

To serve, invert the mousse onto a platter and carefully remove the plastic wrap. If necessary, smooth the top of the mousse with a spatula. Serve with garlic-oregano crostini.

garlic-oregano crostini

¾ cup olive oil

1 tablespoon crumbled dried oregano

1 large garlic clove, minced

½ teaspoon ground chipotle chile

½ teaspoon salt

½ teaspoon freshly ground black pepper

Twenty ⅓-inch-thick baguette slices

This blend of two classic flavors, combined with a hint of chipotle, makes for a fast and easy party favorite. You can make these 3 days ahead and store them in an airtight container.

Preheat the oven to 350°F.

Mix the olive oil, oregano, garlic, ground chipotle, salt, and pepper in a medium bowl to blend. Using a pastry brush, brush the olive oil mixture over the baguette slices, turning to coat both sides. Transfer the slices to a baking sheet and bake for 10 minutes, or until golden brown. Let cool before serving.

ROLLED MUSHROOM TAQUITOS WITH ROASTED TOMATILLO—CILANTRO SALSA

1½ tablespoons olive oil

¾ cup chopped onion

2 garlic cloves, minced

5 ounces button mushrooms, chopped

1½ tablespoons chopped fresh cilantro

Salt and freshly ground black pepper

Twelve 6-inch corn tortillas

Vegetable oil, for panfrying

Roasted Tomatillo–Cilantro Salsa (page 167)

Taquitos, also known as *flautas* where I grew up, are corn tortillas that are stuffed, rolled, and fried. Shredded chicken or beef is the traditional filling, but here I use mushrooms and pair them with a tart tomatillo salsa for a great vegetarian dish.

Heat ½ tablespoon of the olive oil in a large heavy skillet over medium-high heat. Add the onion and garlic and sauté for 5 minutes, or until beginning to brown. Add the remaining 1 tablespoon oil and the mushrooms, and sauté for 5 minutes, or until golden. Remove from the heat. Stir in the cilantro, and season the mushroom filling to taste with salt and pepper.

Place the tortillas on a work surface and spread 2 tablespoons of the filling down the center. Roll them up like a soft taco (into a cylinder). Place a toothpick in the center and one at each end of each taquito to keep the filling from falling out. (These can be made 1 day ahead to this point. Transfer them to baking sheets, cover, and refrigerate.)

Place a medium skillet over medium-high heat, and add enough vegetable oil to reach halfway up the sides of the pan. Heat the oil to 350°F. Working in batches, fry the taquitos until golden brown, about 1 minute per side. Transfer them to paper towels to drain.

Remove the toothpicks from the taquitos, and transfer the taquitos to a platter. Spoon the tomatillo-cilantro salsa down the center of each taquito, and serve.

PUFF PASTRY—WRAPPED JALAPEÑOS STUFFED WITH OAXACA CHEESE

Nonstick cooking spray

2½ cups shredded Oaxaca cheese or mozzarella cheese

1½ tablespoons crumbled dried oregano, preferably Mexican

Salt and freshly ground black pepper

18 jalapeño chiles, charred (see page 35), peeled, stemmed, seeded, and left whole

One 17.3-ounce package frozen puff pastry, thawed

All-purpose flour, for rolling

1 egg, lightly beaten with 1 tablespoon water

These guys are spicy! If you're afraid of the heat, you can use güero chiles, but jalapeños are exactly the right size for an appetizer. Oaxaca cheese, like mozzarella, is a mild-flavored white cheese that is excellent for melting. It's popular for quesadillas in Mexico.

Preheat the oven to 350°F. Spray a large baking sheet with nonstick cooking spray.

Mix the cheese and the oregano in a medium bowl to blend. Season to taste with salt and pepper. Carefully fill each jalapeño with 1 tablespoon of the cheese mixture. (The jalapeños can be prepared 1 day ahead. Transfer the filled jalapeños carefully to a baking sheet, cover, and refrigerate.)

Working with 1 sheet at a time, roll the puff pastry on a lightly floured surface to ¼-inch thickness. Cut it into nine 3 x 4-inch rectangles. Place the rectangles on a work surface, and brush each one lightly with the egg wash. Place 1 jalapeño in the center of each rectangle, on the diagonal. Tightly fold the puff pastry, like an envelope, over the jalapeño to enclose it completely. Brush the pastry lightly with the egg wash. Press the tines of a fork lightly on the seams to seal the pastry. Invert the packets onto the prepared baking sheet so they are seam side down. Brush them lightly with egg wash. Repeat with the remaining puff pastry and jalapeños.

Bake until puffed and golden, about 20 minutes. Let cool for 5 minutes, and then transfer the pastry-wrapped jalapeños to a platter and serve.

MASCARPONE-STUFFED SQUASH BLOSSOMS WITH RASPBERRY VINAIGRETTE

⅓ cup fresh raspberries

⅓ cup chopped shallots

¼ cup raspberry vinegar

½ cup olive oil

Salt and freshly ground black pepper

⅓ cup mascarpone cheese

1 teaspoon minced canned chipotle chiles in adobo sauce

½ teaspoon minced fresh thyme

12 fresh squash blossoms, pistils removed

Vegetable oil, for frying

½ cup all-purpose flour

Beer Batter (page 50)

In Tijuana, as soon as the days get a little warmer, the street vendors start to appear with giant bunches of squash blossoms. I grew up eating squash blossoms sautéed and stuffed in quesadillas, served with fresh raspberries. The addition of mascarpone, an Italian triple-cream cheese, takes the dish to a whole new level.

Combine the raspberries, shallots, and vinegar in a blender or food processor, and process to form a coarse puree. With the machine running, gradually add the olive oil. Season the vinaigrette with salt and black pepper to taste. Set aside.

Mix the mascarpone, chipotle chiles and sauce, and thyme in a small bowl. Season the filling to taste with salt and pepper. Place the filling in a pastry bag fitted with a ¼-inch tip. Pipe the filling into each squash blossom and twist the blossom at the top to enclose it.

Place a medium-size heavy saucepan over medium-high heat and add enough vegetable oil to reach one third of the way up the sides of the pan. Heat the oil to 350°F.

Dust the squash blossoms in the flour and then dip them into the beer batter. Working in batches, fry the squash blossoms for 3 minutes, or until they are golden brown. Transfer them to paper towels to drain. Arrange the squash blossoms on a platter, drizzle with the raspberry vinaigrette, and serve.

TIP NO PASTRY BAG? NO WORRIES. PUT THE FILLING IN A PLASTIC BAG AND CUT A ¼-INCH HOLE IN ONE OF THE CORNERS.

beer batter

1 cup all-purpose flour

1 teaspoon salt

½ teaspoon freshly
ground black pepper

1 cup dark Mexican beer

Crack open a cold Mexican *cerveza,* like a Negra Modelo or a Dos Equis (XX) Amber, to make this tasty beer batter. It will also change the way you think about fried fish.

Mix the flour, salt, and pepper in a medium bowl. Gradually add the beer while whisking. Set the batter aside and let it rest for 15 minutes before using.

SEARED QUESO FRESCO WITH TOMATILLO SALSA AND TORTILLA CHIPS

1 pound tomatillos, husks removed

½ medium onion, chopped

3 serrano chiles, stemmed and seeded

3 garlic cloves, quartered

3 tablespoons finely chopped fresh cilantro

Salt and freshly ground black pepper

1 tablespoon olive oil

1 pound panela cheese (or mozzarella cheese), cut into 1-inch-thick slices, patted dry

Tortilla chips (see Tip)

When you see how easy it is to make this salsa from scratch, you will never want to buy a jar again. And forget bagged chips! It takes almost no effort to make your own at home. In my version of this classic recipe, the cheese is seared (*asado*) rather than deep-fried, resulting in a lighter alternative that really brings out the sweet flavor of the panela cheese. If you don't want to go out of your way to purchase the panela cheese, substitute a moist mozzarella.

Preheat the oven to 375°F.

Put the tomatillos in a medium saucepan and add enough water to cover. Bring to a simmer over medium heat and cook for 5 minutes, or until tender. Transfer the tomatillos and ¼ cup of the cooking liquid to a food processor. Add the onion, chiles, garlic, and cilantro, and blend until smooth. Transfer the salsa to a bowl and let it cool completely. Then season to taste with salt and pepper, cover, and refrigerate until cold. (The salsa can be prepared 1 day ahead and kept refrigerated.)

Heat the olive oil in a large heavy sauté pan over medium-high heat. Working in 2 batches, add the cheese slices and sear for 2 minutes per side, or until browned. Carefully transfer the cheese to a platter. Repeat with the remaining cheese. To eat, top each tortilla chip with a piece of cheese and then with salsa.

TIP TORTILLA CHIPS, OR *TOTOPOS*, AS THEY ARE KNOWN IN MEXICO, ARE VERY EASY TO MAKE. CUT TORTILLAS INTO ANY DESIRED SHAPE (YOU CAN HAVE FUN WITH THIS IF YOU LIKE) AND DEEP-FRY THEM IN 350°F VEGETABLE OIL UNTIL CRISP, ABOUT 3 MINUTES. DRAIN THEM ON PAPER TOWELS AND SEASON THEM HEAVILY WITH SALT WHILE THEY ARE STILL WARM. STORE THE TORTILLA CHIPS IN AN AIRTIGHT CONTAINER AT ROOM TEMPERATURE FOR UP TO 1 DAY.

ANCHO, PECAN, AND HONEY—GLAZED CHICKEN DRUMETTES

½ cup honey

½ cup chopped pecans

3 tablespoons unsalted butter

1 tablespoon distilled white vinegar

1 tablespoon Worcestershire sauce

1 tablespoon ground ancho chile

1 teaspoon garlic powder

Salt and freshly ground black pepper

1½ pounds chicken drumettes

This recipe plays on my favorite combination: spicy and sweet. Don't worry about the chicken drying out in the oven—all of the flavor and juice is sealed in by the crunchy pecan glaze. Drumettes are the part of a chicken wing that, when separated from the rest of the wing, looks like a miniature drumstick. You can carve the wings yourself, ask your butcher to do it, or purchase frozen drumettes in the freezer section of the supermarket (thaw them overnight in the refrigerator).

Preheat the oven to 350°F.

Stir the honey, pecans, and butter in a medium-size heavy saucepan over medium-low heat for 3 minutes, or until the mixture bubbles. Remove from the heat. Stir in the vinegar, Worcestershire sauce, ancho chile, and garlic powder. Season the glaze to taste with salt and black pepper.

Place the chicken drumettes on a baking sheet. Sprinkle with salt and pepper. Brush the drumettes all over with the glaze. Bake for 25 minutes, or until the chicken is cooked through. Serve hot.

GOAT CHEESE TART WITH CHIPOTLE-RASPBERRY CHUTNEY

1 tablespoon vegetable oil

1½ cups chopped onion

6 garlic cloves, thinly sliced

2½ cups chicken broth

1 cup chopped red bell pepper

1 cup honey

1 tablespoon minced peeled fresh ginger

5 tablespoons apple cider vinegar

¼ cup canned chipotle chiles in adobo sauce

One 10-ounce package frozen raspberries, thawed and drained

½ cup chopped fresh cilantro

One 6-ounce container fresh raspberries

Salt and freshly ground black pepper

If you don't want to go through the trouble of baking the puff-pastry tart, just serve this wonderful chutney alongside the goat cheese for your guests to spread on crackers. I always have the chutney on hand to stir into hummus or to slather onto a piece of grilled chicken. The creamy goat cheese is the perfect counterpoint to the smoky-sweet chutney.

Heat the vegetable oil in a large heavy saucepan over medium-high heat. Add the onion and cook for 5 minutes, or until translucent. Add the garlic and cook for 3 more minutes. Add the chicken broth, bell pepper, honey, ginger, vinegar, and chipotle chiles and sauce, and bring to a boil. Reduce the heat to medium-low and simmer for 2½ hours, or until the sauce thickens.

Add the thawed frozen raspberries and cook, stirring occasionally, for 15 minutes. Remove the pan from the heat and let the chutney cool slightly. Then stir in the cilantro and the fresh raspberries. Season to taste with salt and black pepper. (The chutney can be prepared 3 days ahead. Cool, then cover and refrigerate.)

Preheat the oven to 400°F. Line a baking sheet with parchment paper.

1 sheet frozen puff pastry (half of a 17.3-ounce package), thawed (see Tip)

All-purpose flour, for rolling

1 large egg, lightly beaten

One 5.5-ounce log soft fresh goat cheese, at room temperature

Roll out the puff pastry on a lightly floured surface to form a 12 x 15-inch rectangle. Cut one 12 x 5-inch rectangle, two 11 x ½-inch strips, and two 5 x ½-inch strips from the pastry.

Place the rectangle on the prepared baking sheet. Pierce it all over with a fork. Using a pastry brush, brush all of the strips with the beaten egg. Place the short strips, egg side down, on the short ends of the pastry rectangle to form a raised edge. Place the long strips, egg side down, along the long sides of the pastry.

Bake the tart shell until golden, about 15 minutes. Keep the oven on.

Spread the goat cheese evenly over the bottom of the hot tart shell, and return it to the oven. Bake for 5 minutes, or until the cheese begins to melt. Cut the tart into 1-inch-wide slices, top each one with a generous dollop of the chipotle-raspberry chutney, and serve.

TIP ALWAYS USE AN ALL-BUTTER PUFF PASTRY FOR THE BEST FLAVOR AND RESULTS.

THE DUCK BURRITO

1 tablespoon salt

4 garlic cloves, smashed

2 shallots, sliced

6 fresh thyme sprigs

2 small fresh rosemary sprigs

One 5-pound whole duck, split into 6 pieces (2 legs, 2 thighs, and 2 breasts)

Freshly ground black pepper

4 cups duck fat (or 2 cups lard plus 2 cups duck fat)

Six to eight 10-inch flour tortillas, warmed (see page 59)

3 scallions (white and pale green parts only), cut into matchstick-size strips

Roasted Tomatillo–Cilantro Salsa (page 167)

This is the best burrito you will ever taste in your entire life, and that's no exaggeration. To "confit" is to preserve the duck meat by first curing it in salt, then cooking and storing it in its own fat. This is one of those things that I eat only on occasion, for obvious reasons, but look forward to tremendously. Take into consideration that the duck must be prepared a day ahead—but believe me, it's worth the extra effort. (You could also buy duck confit already made to cut the prep time way down.) I must confess to you that, on occasion, I've used lard from a local butcher when I don't have enough duck fat (which I buy at Whole Foods), with the response from my uninformed family usually being, "Marcela, the duck tastes different today. It tastes . . . better."

Sprinkle ½ tablespoon of the salt over the bottom of a 9 x 13-inch glass baking dish (or any container large enough to hold the duck pieces snugly in a single layer). Scatter half of the garlic, shallots, thyme, and rosemary in the dish. Arrange the duck pieces, skin side up, on top of the salt mixture. Then sprinkle the duck with the remaining salt, garlic, shallots, thyme, and rosemary and a little black pepper. Cover tightly with plastic wrap and refrigerate for 1 day.

Place the duck fat in a medium-size heavy saucepan and stir over medium-low heat until completely rendered.

Preheat the oven to 225°F.

Remove the baking dish from the refrigerator. Pick off and reserve the garlic cloves. Using cold running water, rinse the

RECIPE CONTINUES

duck pieces (discarding the shallots, thyme, and rosemary) and pat them dry. Arrange the duck pieces and the reserved garlic cloves in a single snug layer in a large, wide ovenproof pot. Pour the melted fat over the duck (the pieces should be covered by fat) and place in the oven. Cook, uncovered, for 2½ hours, or until the duck is tender and can be easily pulled from the bone.

Remove from the oven and allow to cool slightly. Then remove the duck pieces from the fat. (Cool the fat completely, then cover and refrigerate for another use.) Remove all of the meat from the bones, and discard the skin and bones. Shred the duck meat. (Duck confit will keep in the refrigerator for up to 6 months. To store, return the shredded duck to the fat, cool completely, and then refrigerate. To reheat, stir the shredded duck in its fat over medium heat until the fat melts completely. Cool slightly. Remove the shredded duck from the fat.)

Place 1 tortilla on a work surface. Spoon a generous amount of shredded duck confit down the center, and sprinkle some scallions on top. Roll up like a soft taco, into a cylinder. Trim the edges and cut the burrito in half crosswise. Cut the halves on the diagonal, and arrange them standing upright, on a platter. Repeat with the remaining tortillas, duck confit, and scallions. Serve with the tomatillo-cilantro salsa for dipping.

WARMING TORTILLAS

You could end up in the middle of a very heated discussion if you ask two Mexicans the proper way to warm a tortilla. Many do it over a *comal* (a large heavy sauté pan), but I grew up in a house where both corn and flour tortillas were warmed directly over a gas burner. We would turn them constantly until they were perfectly soft and ready to roll, about 30 seconds. (Now, if you're lucky enough to find freshly baked and still-warm tortillas, as I sometimes do at the corner store, there's no need to warm them.) The point is to make the tortillas pliable so they won't crack or break while rolling.

GRILLED SPICY QUAIL

⅔ cup canola oil

¼ cup freshly grated Parmesan cheese

¼ cup white wine vinegar

2 tablespoons Chile-Italian Seasoning (recipe follows)

8 semiboneless quail (torso bones removed, but bird is still whole)

Salt and freshly ground black pepper

Lime wedges, for serving

My dad used to hunt, and quail was his favorite game, so grilled quail regularly appeared on our dinner table. When pressed for time, my mom would marinate the quail in store-bought Italian dressing spiced up with chile powder, grill it, and serve it as an appetizer followed by *carne asada.* In this recipe, I create the marinade from scratch, with just the right amount of chile powder. Squeeze a lime over the quail and don't be afraid to eat it with your hands—it's messy but delicious! This marinade is also great with chicken.

To make the marinade, whisk the canola oil, Parmesan cheese, vinegar, chile-Italian seasoning, and 2 tablespoons water in a small bowl.

Rinse the quail and pat dry. Arrange the quail in a baking dish that is large enough to hold them in one layer, and add the marinade, turning the quail to coat them well. Cover and marinate in the refrigerator, turning the quail once or twice, for at least 1 day and up to 2 days.

Remove the quail from the refrigerator and bring to room temperature (about 30 minutes). Prepare a grill to medium-high heat, or heat a grill pan over medium-high heat.

Remove the quail from the marinade (discard the marinade), and pat dry with paper towels. Season the quail with salt and pepper, and grill for 3 to 4 minutes on each side, or until just cooked through. The meat should still be slightly pink in the center. Serve with lime wedges.

chile-italian seasoning

2 tablespoons crumbled dried oregano

1 tablespoon dried parsley

1 teaspoon dried basil

1/4 teaspoon dried thyme

1 tablespoon salt

1 tablespoon garlic salt

1/4 teaspoon celery salt

1 tablespoon onion powder

1 tablespoon sugar

2 teaspoons Anaheim chile powder

1 teaspoon freshly ground black pepper

This smoky rub has endless possibilities: sprinkle it on potatoes before roasting, rub it on chicken breasts before grilling, or use it to season steaks before searing or halibut before roasting. For a garnish, mix a couple of tablespoons of this spice mix with half a cup of crème fraîche and drizzle it over soups.

Combine the oregano, parsley, basil, thyme, salt, garlic salt, celery salt, onion powder, sugar, chile powder, and pepper in a glass jar. Screw the lid on tightly, and shake until the mixture is well blended. Store at room temperature for up to 6 months.

SOUPS & SALADS

MI MERCADO, TU MERCADO

Because they usually involve relatively few ingredients and a short amount of time in the kitchen, a soup's or a salad's success relies mostly on the quality of its ingredients. Luckily for me, I've had the privilege of growing up in Tijuana, right on the U.S.–Mexico border, where endless varieties of fresh fruit and produce, as well as seafood, meats and poultry, chiles, and exotic ingredients, are all within a 15-mile radius of my home. Needless to say, the sleek supermarkets of San Diego and the thriving street markets of Tijuana provide two very different kinds of grocery-shopping experiences. The greatest thing about growing up smack on the border of two different countries is the access you have to both worlds—not only to the ingredients to cook with but also to both cultures.

I cross the international border to grocery-shop when I need a veal shank, frozen puff pastry, fine French cheese, and any of the many ingredients I am accustomed to cooking with that have not found their way into the Mexican markets, probably because of their higher cost. (Or maybe because they just wouldn't sell, regardless of their price. Little Italy in downtown San Diego is the place to go when I need fresh gnocchi, but it's best if it stays there because the poor little gnocchi would dry out before anybody bought them in Tijuana!)

Shopping in San Diego is a delightful experience—everything is so organized. The supermarket is at the perfect temperature (sometimes I even walk a little slower down the grocery aisles before venturing out into the summer heat). Everything is precisely labeled. Signage leads you to every ingredient. You can find frozen everything: ready-made dinners, pastries, vegetables, fruits . . . Fresh fruits and vegetables come in from all over the world, putting all sorts of ingredients at your fingertips. How could I run into a tower of gorgeous golden beets in one aisle and then an array of imported cheeses in the next and not dream up the Golden Beet Carpaccio with Gorgonzola and Chile Oil (page 83)?

Then there are the street markets in Tijuana. You can find American-style markets in most cities in Mexico, but to get a true feeling of the local color you must visit a *mercado.* I go to Tijuana's Mercado Hidalgo every Monday. It's divided into about eighty different stalls where you can find anything from piñatas, Mexican candy, fresh produce, any kind of chile (seriously, there are too many to count, both fresh and dry), exotic fruits, salted plums, and chile-coated dried mango to fireworks and cooking utensils like *molcajetes,* hot-chocolate frothers, and tortilla presses.

Dried fish and candied fruits (and even sweet potatoes), hibiscus leaves, tamarind pods, and ceramics are all lined up in the *mercado.* There are taco stands and shops with holistic herbs and remedies as well as plenty of *artesanias* (Mexican crafts). Heck, you can even visit the market's chapel honoring the Virgen de Guadalupe, Mexico's representation of the Virgin Mary. It's like a small city! And it's guaranteed you'll find fresh banana leaves every time you need them. My list for the Tijuana market might include fresh chiles, squash blossoms, quail eggs, or just a couple of things that I'll be needing that week, but I always end up going home with so much more.

The market, or the supermarket as it may be, is where I sort my thoughts, seek inspiration, and find the perfect seasonal items to make each dish worth serving to my friends and family. Access to two incredible different food worlds has greatly influenced my cooking. For these soups and salads—or any of my recipes, really—I strongly suggest that you use the freshest ingredients you can find. Most likely, it won't require crossing an international border. But if it does, and you can, consider yourself lucky.

BUTTERNUT SQUASH— CHIPOTLE BISQUE

1 medium butternut squash

3 tablespoons olive oil

1½ cups chopped onion

½ cup chopped celery

½ cup chopped carrot

2 garlic cloves, minced

6 cups chicken broth

Salt

3 teaspoons minced canned chipotle chiles in adobo sauce

½ cup Mexican *crema* (see page 70) or sour cream

Freshly ground black pepper

While winter squash and pumpkins aren't usually associated with Mexican food, they are actually found in many dishes across the country, especially in Oaxaca. The candied flesh is used in desserts, and its seeds are used in sauces called *pipiáns*. This recipe utilizes both the flesh of butternut squash, which is roasted until it caramelizes, and the seeds, which are toasted for a crunchy garnish. Serve this hearty bisque for dinner on a cool autumn night, or pour it into individual shot glasses for a savvy appetizer.

Preheat the oven to 400°F.

Cut the squash in half lengthwise. Scoop out the seeds, discarding as much stringy pulp as possible, put them in a sieve, and rinse them under cold running water. Set the seeds aside.

Using 1 tablespoon of the olive oil, grease a glass baking dish. Place the butternut squash in the dish, cut side down. Pierce the squash all over with a fork. Roast for 45 minutes, or until very tender. Let it cool.

Heat the remaining 2 tablespoons oil in a large heavy pot over medium-high heat. Add the onion, celery, and carrot. Sauté for 10 minutes, or until just tender. Add the garlic and sauté for 2 minutes. Scoop the flesh of the butternut squash into the pot and stir. Add the chicken broth and bring to a

RECIPE CONTINUES

TIP DID YOU KNOW THAT CHIPOTLE CHILES ARE DRIED SMOKED JALAPEÑOS? THE HEAT OF CANNED CHIPOTLES VARIES BY BRAND. IF THEY ARE TOO SPICY FOR YOUR TASTE BUDS, USE THE ADOBO SAUCE THAT ACCOMPANIES THEM INSTEAD.

boil. Reduce the heat to low, cover the pot, and simmer for 30 minutes, or until the vegetables are very tender.

Meanwhile, heat a small pan over medium-low heat. Add the reserved squash seeds and toast, stirring occasionally, for 30 minutes, or until crunchy. Season the seeds heavily with salt. Set them aside to cool.

Let the soup cool slightly, and then puree it in batches in a blender until very smooth. Return the soup to the pot and keep it warm over medium-low heat. Mix in 2 teaspoons of the chipotle.

Stir the *crema* and the remaining 1 teaspoon chipotle together in a small bowl. Season the chipotle cream with salt and pepper.

Transfer the bisque to individual bowls, and top each serving with a dollop of chipotle cream and a sprinkling of toasted squash seeds.

CREMA

Mexican *crema* is Mexico's version of crème fraîche, unpasteurized fresh cream thickened by naturally occurring bacteria. *Crema* is used as a topping in many dishes in Mexico, such as tostadas, enchiladas, chilaquiles, and moles. Because it is unpasteurized, you won't find the real thing on this side of the border, but the pasteurized Mexican *cremas* in your grocery store are fine for drizzling over finished dishes, as is sour cream.

MANCHEGO AND POBLANO SOUP

14 poblano chiles, stemmed and seeded

½ medium onion, coarsely chopped

2 garlic cloves, coarsely chopped

8 tablespoons (1 stick) unsalted butter

2 tablespoons all-purpose flour

4 cups whole milk

1 cup grated Manchego cheese (or Monterey Jack cheese)

Salt and freshly ground black pepper

1 cup diced Manchego cheese (or Monterey Jack cheese)

1 medium russet potato, boiled, peeled, and cut into cubes

3 corn tostadas (see Tips, page 23), grilled and broken into pieces

Manchego, a mild-flavored Spanish cheese, makes this classic Mexican soup a hit. As good as this is when served as a starter, it is also great paired with water crackers for the perfect pre-dinner snack or boiled down until thickened and transformed into an alfredo-like sauce for pasta or poultry. All told, you need to buy about 3 ounces Manchego for this recipe.

Bring a medium-size heavy saucepan of salted water to a boil. Add the poblanos and cook for 20 minutes, or until tender. Drain the poblanos and transfer them to a blender. Add the onion, garlic, and ¼ cup water. Blend until smooth. Set aside.

Melt the butter in a large heavy pot over medium-high heat. Whisk in the flour and cook for 3 minutes, whisking constantly (do not brown). Reduce the heat to medium and whisk in the chile mixture. Cook, whisking, for 4 minutes, or until slightly thickened. Whisk in the milk. Bring the soup to a simmer and cook, whisking every minute or so to prevent scorching, for 10 minutes, or until slightly thickened.

Whisk in the grated Manchego cheese. Season the soup to taste with salt and pepper.

Transfer the soup to bowls, and top with the diced cheese and the potato cubes, and then with the tostadas.

CHILLED AVOCADO SOUP WITH SCALLOPS

3 tablespoons olive oil

1 cup diced white onion

1 serrano chile, stemmed, seeded, and diced

3 garlic cloves, minced

Salt

4 firm but ripe avocados, halved, pitted, and peeled

2 cups chicken broth

5 tablespoons fresh lemon juice

¼ cup chopped fresh cilantro

Freshly ground black pepper

6 to 8 jumbo scallops

½ cup Mexican crema (see page 70) or crème fraîche, whisked to soften

Avocado gives this dairy-free soup its creamy texture. For a super-sophisticated presentation, serve it in chilled martini glasses and garnish each one with a drizzle of Mexican crema or crème fraîche. If you prefer a soup with a thinner consistency, add water until it's exactly the way you like it.

Heat 2 tablespoons of the olive oil in a medium skillet over medium heat. Add the onion and serrano chile and sauté for 10 minutes, or until tender. Add the garlic and cook for 2 minutes. Season with salt. Remove from the heat and set aside to cool.

Put the avocados in a blender. Add the chicken broth, lemon juice, cilantro, and onion mixture. Puree until smooth. Blend in 2 cups water. Strain the soup into a large bowl, and season it to taste with salt and pepper. Cover and refrigerate until well chilled, about 3 hours.

Sprinkle the scallops all over with salt and pepper. Heat the remaining 1 tablespoon olive oil in a skillet over medium-high heat. Working in 2 batches, sear the scallops for 1 minute per side, or until just cooked through.

Pour the chilled soup into individual bowls. Top each serving with a scallop, and drizzle with the crema.

GRILLED CORN AND POBLANO POTATO SALAD

This is great served with grilled flank steak and ice-cold beer or lemonade. Stuck indoors? A grill pan for the corn yields an equally delicious summer salad.

3 ears fresh corn, husks removed

2 pounds medium red-skinned potatoes

2 poblano chiles, charred (see page 35), peeled, stemmed, seeded, and chopped

1 cup chopped scallions (white and pale green parts only)

½ cup sour cream

¼ cup mayonnaise

¼ cup chopped fresh cilantro

Salt and freshly ground black pepper

Put the potatoes in a large pot and add salted water to cover. Bring to a boil and cook for 30 minutes, or until tender when pierced with a knife. Drain the potatoes and let them cool slightly.

Meanwhile, prepare a grill or grill pan to medium-high heat. Add the corn and grill, turning the ears, until evenly browned on all sides, 10 minutes.

Halve the potatoes and put them in a large bowl. Using a sharp knife, carefully cut the kernels off the corncobs and add the kernels to the bowl. Add the poblano chiles, scallions, sour cream, mayonnaise, and cilantro, and fold together. Season the potato salad to taste with salt and pepper. (The potato salad can be made 1 day ahead and refrigerated. Let it stand at room temperature for 30 minutes before serving.)

MANGO, PAPAYA, SHRIMP, AND CRAB SALAD IN HONEYDEW CUPS

6 tablespoons mayonnaise

¼ cup (packed) light
brown sugar

¼ cup chopped fresh
cilantro

3 tablespoons Dijon
mustard

3 tablespoons distilled
white vinegar

1 tablespoon minced
seeded jalapeño chile

2 teaspoons fresh lime
juice

1 teaspoon bottled hot
sauce (such as Huichol)

Salt and freshly ground
black pepper

2 cups diced papaya
(from 1 small papaya)

2 cups diced mango (from
2 large mangoes)

1 pound cooked shrimp,
shelled, deveined, and
diced

8 ounces lump crabmeat,
picked over to remove
any shell and cartilage

2 to 3 small honeydew
melons (see Tip)

This refreshing seafood salad is inspired by one I had at an outdoor café in Yucatán, where the cuisine is influenced by Mayan, Caribbean, Mexican, French, and Middle Eastern cultures. Mango and papaya add unexpected sweetness and a tropical twist. I make it for brunch with friends, and serve it with tall glasses of guava iced tea.

Combine the mayonnaise, brown sugar, cilantro, mustard, vinegar, jalapeño, lime juice, and hot sauce in a medium bowl and stir well. Season the dressing to taste with salt and pepper.

Put the papaya, mango, shrimp, and crabmeat in a large bowl. Add the dressing and toss gently to combine.

Halve the melons and scoop out the seeds. Spoon the salad into the honeydew cups, and serve.

TIP THE BOTTOMS OF THE HONEYDEW HALVES MAY NEED TO BE PARTLY SLICED OFF SO THEY DON'T ROLL AROUND. AN AVERAGE HONEYDEW IS ABOUT THE SIZE OF A SMALL BOWL ON THE INSIDE.

WHITE BEAN AND GRILLED OCTOPUS SALAD

1 pound baby octopus, tentacles attached

¼ cup plus ⅓ cup olive oil

3 garlic cloves, minced

½ lime

Salt and freshly ground black pepper

3 cups cooked great northern or pinto beans

2 tablespoons chopped scallions (white and pale green parts only)

2 tablespoons fresh lime juice

3 tablespoons chopped fresh cilantro

1 tablespoon dried oregano

This dish, popular in northern Mexico, is a summer favorite at my house and tastes great with any grilled seafood, not just octopus. Freshly cooked beans are always best, but you can substitute canned beans; just be sure to rinse them thoroughly. You'll need two 14-ounce cans here.

Prepare a grill to medium-high heat, or heat a grill pan over medium-high heat.

Mix the octopus, the ¼ cup olive oil, and the garlic in a medium bowl. Squeeze the lime half over it, sprinkle with salt and pepper, and let stand for 30 minutes.

Grill the octopus, turning it once, for 3 minutes, or until just cooked through.

Mix the warm octopus, beans, scallions, lime juice, cilantro, oregano, and remaining ⅓ cup olive oil in a large bowl. Season to taste with salt and pepper. Serve warm.

JÍCAMA, BEET, AND ÁRBOL CHILE SLAW

¼ cup soy sauce

3 tablespoons fresh lime juice

1 tablespoon toasted sesame oil

2 teaspoons balsamic vinegar

1 tablespoon sugar

1 fresh árbol chile, stemmed, seeded, and cut into rings

Salt and freshly ground black pepper

2 cups shredded peeled jícama (from 1 small jícama)

3 medium raw beets, peeled and shredded

1 cup thinly sliced peeled seeded cucumber

Jícama, a Mexican root vegetable with the crispness of a raw potato, but with a sweeter taste, adds great crunch to this simple salad, which gets a lift from the unexpected addition of soy sauce and sesame oil to the dressing. My great-grandmother used beet coloring as lipstick and as blush. Here I add beets not only for their vibrant color but also for crunch.

Mix the soy sauce, lime juice, sesame oil, balsamic vinegar, sugar, and árbol chile in a medium bowl. Season the dressing to taste with salt and pepper. Toss the jícama, beets, and cucumber with the dressing to combine. Cover and refrigerate until chilled. Serve cold.

CUCUMBERS AND RADISHES SPRINKLED WITH LIME

Six 1-inch pink radishes, trimmed and thinly sliced

1 cucumber, peeled and thinly sliced

3 limes, halved

Salt

1 bunch arugula

1 tablespoon olive oil

Freshly ground black pepper

This has to be the easiest recipe in the book. Maybe that's why this plate showed up on the table almost every day when I was growing up. It also happens to be a very healthy and refreshing snack that my son loves. At every taco stand across Mexico, next to the salsas, you will find a bowl of sliced cucumbers and another with whole or halved radishes. These are meant to be sprinkled with lime juice and a little bit of salt to appease your hunger while the tacos are being prepared. Make sure both the radishes and the cucumbers are very fresh and crisp!

Arrange the radish and cucumber slices, overlapping, on a round platter. Squeeze the juice from 2 of the limes over the vegetables, and season with salt. Mound the arugula in the center of the platter, atop the cucumbers and radishes. Squeeze the juice from the remaining lime over the arugula and drizzle with the olive oil. Sprinkle the arugula with salt and pepper, and serve.

CACTUS SALAD WITH AVOCADO DRESSING

¼ onion

2 garlic cloves, mashed with the side of a knife

1 teaspoon crumbled dried oregano

Salt

1½ pounds cleaned prickly pear cactus paddles, chopped (about 6 cups)

1 avocado, halved, pitted, and peeled

¼ cup (packed) fresh cilantro leaves, plus ¼ cup chopped fresh cilantro

3 tablespoons extra-virgin olive oil

½ serrano chile, stemmed and seeded

1½ tablespoons distilled white vinegar

Freshly ground black pepper

½ cup chopped seeded plum tomatoes

½ cup crumbled queso fresco or feta cheese

⅓ cup chopped scallions (white and pale green parts only)

1 cup chicharrón pieces

This is one of my favorite salads—it is a perfect accompaniment to most traditional Mexican dishes. Serve it with Cochinita Pibil (page 126) or a *carne asada.* In Mexico the chicharrones (crackling pork rinds) are sold packaged like potato chips, or in larger pieces at street stands, and are eaten as a snack—on their own or sprinkled with lime juice and bottled hot sauce. Here they provide a nice crunch. Make sure to add them at the end because they will get soggy if they sit too long in the dressing. If you want to keep the salad light and healthy, leave the chicharrones out altogether.

Combine the onion, garlic, oregano, ½ teaspoon salt, and 4 cups water in a large heavy saucepan, and bring to a boil over high heat. Add the cactus and boil for 7 minutes, or until tender and no longer bright green. Strain the cactus and discard the onion and garlic. Cool completely. (The cactus can be prepared 1 day ahead. Cover and refrigerate.)

Put the avocado, cilantro leaves, olive oil, serrano chile, vinegar, and 2 tablespoons water in a blender. Blend until very smooth (the dressing will be thick). Season to taste with salt and black pepper.

Transfer the cactus to a large bowl and add the tomatoes, queso fresco, scallions, and chopped cilantro. Toss to combine. Add enough dressing to coat, and toss gently. Divide the salad among 4 plates, and top each serving with chicharrones.

GOLDEN BEET CARPACCIO WITH GORGONZOLA AND CHILE OIL

1 large golden beet (about 12 ounces), trimmed

⅓ cup olive oil

1 red jalapeño chile, stemmed, seeded, and minced

1 tablespoon distilled white vinegar

Salt and freshly ground black pepper

⅓ cup crumbled Gorgonzola cheese

This is one of those recipes where success relies on the freshness of the ingredients. Use the best-quality Gorgonzola you can find, be it a mild domestic version or the more pungent Italian variety. Either one will pair nicely with the chile oil, which enlivens this classic recipe. This makes for a beautiful presentation on a platter, but you can easily divide the beet slices among individual plates and serve it that way.

Preheat the oven to 400°F.

Wrap the beet tightly in foil. Place the beet directly on the oven rack and roast it for 40 minutes, or until just tender when pierced with a knife. Unwrap it, let it cool to room temperature, and then refrigerate it until completely chilled. (The beet can be roasted 1 day ahead. Wrap it in plastic wrap and refrigerate.)

Combine the olive oil and the minced chile in a small saucepan set over medium-high heat. As soon as the chile begins to sizzle and turns orange, remove the pan from the heat. Transfer the chile oil to a small bowl and let it cool completely. (The chile oil can be made 1 day ahead. Keep covered at room temperature.)

Carefully peel the beet. Using a mandoline set at ⅛-inch thickness, or a very sharp knife, cut the beet into paper-thin rounds. Arrange the beet slices, overlapping, on a large platter. Sprinkle the vinegar all over. Drizzle some of the chile oil (including the minced chile) all over the beets. Season the beet slices generously with salt and pepper. Sprinkle the Gorgonzola over the beets, and serve.

LOBSTER, MANGO, AND AVOCADO SALAD

Two 1¼- to 1½-pound live spiny lobsters or Maine lobsters

¼ cup extra-virgin olive oil

2 teaspoons finely chopped scallion (white and pale green parts only)

1 tablespoon fresh lime juice

2 ruby-red grapefruits

2 firm but ripe avocados, halved, pitted, peeled, and diced

1 mango, peeled, pitted, and diced

4 cups mixed mesclun salad greens

Salt and freshly ground black pepper

Spiny lobster is abundant in the state of Baja and also happens to be one of my dad's favorite foods. He would often come home with plenty for my mom and me to prepare, and on hot days this refreshing salad was a must. The mango brings out the lobster's natural sweetness, and the bright lime juice makes this a perfect summer dish.

Bring a large pot of salted water to a boil. Add the lobsters and boil for 7 minutes, or until cooked through. Drain the lobsters and let them cool completely. When the lobsters are cool enough to handle, remove the meat from the tail (and from the claws if using Maine lobsters), keeping the meat intact. Discard the tomalley, any roe, and shells. Chill the lobster, covered, until cold, at least 1 hour.

Chop the lobster into bite-size pieces. In a small bowl, whisk together the olive oil, scallions, and lime juice; set the dressing aside.

Using a sharp knife, remove the peel and white pith from each grapefruit. Working over a small bowl, cut between the membranes to release the grapefruit segments, letting the juice and segments fall into the bowl. Use a slotted spoon to transfer the segments to a large bowl. Add the lobster, avocados, mango, and mesclun greens.

Whisk the reserved grapefruit juice into the scallion dressing, and season to taste with salt and pepper. Gently toss the salad with dressing to coat. Serve.

MARTHA'S CHICKEN SALAD SANDWICHES

4 cups shredded cooked chicken (from one 2-pound roast chicken)

½ cup minced celery

¼ cup plus 2 tablespoons mayonnaise (or Homemade Chipotle Mayo, page 187)

¼ cup minced seeded canned pickled jalapeño chiles

¼ cup minced pitted kalamata olives

3 tablespoons sour cream

3 tablespoons capers, drained

2 teaspoons bottled hot sauce (such as Huichol)

1 teaspoon Maggi seasoning sauce (see page 28)

½ cup plus 2 tablespoons sesame seeds, toasted (see Tips, page 23)

Salt and freshly ground black pepper

1 rectangular loaf white bread, sliced

I borrowed a page from one of the masters, Martha Stewart, for the presentation of these chicken salad sandwiches, but the recipe is all mine. Mexican and Mediterranean ingredients put a spicy spin on a traditional lunchtime favorite. Think Martha—but with a kick.

Place the chicken, celery, ¼ cup mayonnaise, jalapeño chiles, olives, sour cream, capers, hot sauce, and Maggi sauce in a large bowl and fold to combine. Mix in the 2 tablespoons sesame seeds. Season the chicken salad to taste with salt and pepper. (The chicken salad can be made 2 days ahead. Cover and refrigerate.)

Spread an even layer of chicken salad over half of the slices of bread. Top with the other half of the slices to make sandwiches. Trim the crusts. Cut each sandwich in half on the diagonal.

To serve, arrange the sandwiches, long edge down, in a row on a platter—it will look like the roof of a long house. Spread one side of the "roof" with the remaining 2 tablespoons mayonnaise. Sprinkle the remaining ½ cup sesame seeds over the mayonnaise.

ENTREES

LOS DOS PEDROS

I am occasionally asked who has had the greatest influence on my career as a chef. I certainly owe a debt of gratitude to a number of people. My instructors at the Ritz-Escoffier cooking school in Paris; the editors at *Bon Appétit;* and my grandfather and my aunt Marcela, who were also chefs, are the first to come to mind. But the title of greatest influence goes to two of the best cooks I know, Pedro Huerta and Pedro Rocha, also known by my family as "Los Dos Pedros" (The Two Pedros).

I don't remember exactly what month or year it was when it happened, but one day when I was young my mom decided she didn't want to cook anymore, which was incredibly sad because my mother was an excellent cook. She suffered from a medical condition that made her tire quickly, and cooking became too demanding (kids and carpools, I'm beginning to understand, suck the energy right out of you by the time the first half of the day is over). But our family still needed to eat.

My father rarely treaded on Mom's turf. He brought home the bacon and she cooked it, and that was that. I think he'd sooner die of starvation than make himself a sandwich—the man just doesn't cook. But something needed to be done. In the meantime, my father began eating out a lot. And by a lot, I mean breakfast, lunch, and dinner in a restaurant every day of the week, as well as bringing back plenty of food for the rest of us. Realizing what an incredible waste of money this was, my dad decided he was going to hire the cook from his favorite restaurant, which at the time was the Club Campestre, a country club in Tijuana.

Before you start imagining me living in a palace with servants catering to our every whim and a personal chef making chilaquiles on the spot, remember, this is Tijuana and the cost of labor—along with everything else, really—is much, much cheaper than in the United States. (Why do you think I still live here?)

Anyway, that's how Pedro Huerta came to cook at my house. Pedro wasn't a trained chef. He'd never gone to cooking school and he never worked under any big shot in the culinary world, but boy could he cook. And he was completely unfazed by even the most daunting requests, like my father calling him at noon to request a meal for himself and eight friends.

Meal schedules are different in Mexico. It's usually an early breakfast, a large meal in the middle of the day (*la comida*), and then a light dinner. A call from my father to Pedro at noon meant that food should be on the table at three o'clock. In those three hours, Pedro shopped for all of the ingredients and prepared the meal for my dad, his friends, my mom, and my siblings. His go-to meal on these special occasions was herb-crusted prime rib served with a red wine reduction and mushroom sauce alongside giant spiny lobster halves that were panfried in lots of butter. For sides, some of his best were asparagus with slivered prosciutto and almonds and a huge baked potato. Dessert was always candied figs, which my dad brought home from his plantation in San Quintín, with vanilla bean ice cream. At the end of Pedro's meals, my father and his friends would (literally) applaud his efforts.

I learned a lot from Pedro Huerta, and I was very sad when he left to open his own restaurant. Fortunately, it is four blocks away from my dad's house, so Pedro is still close by when my dad has a longing for perfectly cooked prime rib.

So there we were again, hungry, but with no one to cook for us. We had fallen in love with Pedro, so the only solution was to go out and find another Pedro. Literally. My dad put an ad in the paper looking for a personal chef. He chose Pedro Rocha.

Pedro Rocha, or "El Pedro Nuevo" (The New Pedro) as he was known at my house, came from a seafood restaurant, so his forte was anything from the sea. I'd eaten seafood my whole life, but this Pedro opened my eyes to how seafood should be prepared. El Pedro Nuevo was all about going to the fish market and picking out the freshest seafood and putting it on the table the most organic way possible. Nothing fussy, very few seasonings—just perfectly cooked seafood on the table in record time. He was a master at ceviche and he made incredible seafood appetizers. His *sarandeado* fish, a whole fish cooked in a grill basket, was spectacular and soon became a favorite with my dad's friends. But just like the old Pedro, the new Pedro had to follow his dreams and off he went to work in a restaurant.

The days of having a personal cook were over. With all of us out of the house and with my mom no longer with us, it just didn't make sense anymore—so my father resorted to his old ways, and most of his meals are now again eaten with friends at restaurants (although he occasionally surprises me by knocking on my door at 7 a.m. to ask for huevos rancheros).

As for the two Pedros, there was no way my dad was going to let them go that easily. Every once in a while my dad will relive the old days and invite his friends to the house for a meal created by not one but *both* of our beloved Pedros! Their strengths play off each other to create a menu that is in perfect harmony, and we are privileged to partake in meals that they are now well known for in Tijuana.

I relish these meals for two reasons. Number one: I'm not cooking. I get to chill and eat the foods I grew up with and enjoy a Don Julio 1942 tequila while doing so. Number two: I learn something new from these guys every time I watch them cook. To watch them sitting in silence in the kitchen waiting for the reaction from my dad and his friends, and to hear that reaction—the murmurs of appreciation between bites of an exquisite meal—is an inspiration.

The biggest lesson I've learned from the two Pedros is that you don't need a certificate from the best culinary school in the world, or a Michelin star, or to work under a famous French chef to make memorable food. You just need to have *sazón*—that special touch that makes your food unique—and the ability to cook with so much heart that it garners applause at the end of the meal. Some people learn it in school, and some, like the two Pedros, are born with it.

If I'm ever lucky enough to have someone write about me and my cooking, I hope they describe me as being born with the ability. Thank you, Pedro Rocha and Pedro Huerta: you are masters of your craft. Thank you for sharing your recipes with me, as they were the inspiration for many of the recipes in this book, especially in this chapter. No good-byes, though—my dad has a *comida* next week. I'll see you both there!

MAHIMAHI SMOKED IN BANANA LEAVES

MAHIMAHI SMOKED IN BANANA LEAVES

8 tablespoons (1 stick) unsalted butter, softened

1 tablespoon chopped fresh cilantro

Salt and freshly ground black pepper

Six 12 x 12-inch squares of banana leaf (see opposite)

Six 6-ounce mahimahi fillets

18 very thin lime slices (from 2 limes)

Mango, Serrano, and Avocado Salsa (page 182)

This dish comes with a stranger-than-fiction true story shared with me by a guest on my television show on Discovery en Español. This man's grandfather was once stranded on an island, close to starvation. To survive, he caught a barracuda, wrapped it in seaweed, and cooked it over an open fire. The grandfather lived—and so did the recipe, with a few adaptations for non-life-threatening situations. The banana leaves add subtle flavor to the mahimahi and they look great on the plate. You can find them, fresh or frozen, at most Latin markets. Aluminum foil will also work in their place.

Mix the butter and cilantro together in a small bowl. Season to taste with salt and pepper. Place a piece of plastic wrap on a work surface, and spoon the cilantro butter onto the center. Roll the butter into a 1-inch-thick log and refrigerate it until solid, 2 hours (or for up 2 days).

Prepare an outdoor grill to medium-high heat.

Cut the log of butter into 18 thin rounds.

Place the banana leaf pieces on the grill and cook until they are opaque and pliable, about 1 minute per side. Meanwhile, season the fish all over with salt and pepper.

Place 1 piece of fish in the center of each banana leaf. Top each with 3 rounds of the cilantro butter and 3 lime slices. Fold the banana leaf over the fish to enclose it completely. Tie a small piece of kitchen string around the banana leaf to keep the fish fillet inside.

Grill the fish in the banana leaves for 8 to 10 minutes per side, or until cooked through. Transfer each packet to a plate. Open the packets carefully, top the fish with the salsa, and serve immediately.

BANANA LEAVES

Lush banana leaves, which stand about 5 feet tall as part of the banana plant, are used extensively in Mexico, wrapping everything from fish to tamales. In Asian and Indian cooking they are used for steaming meats, as wraps for smaller bites, and sometimes in lieu of a plate for serving food (Indians believe banana leaves add a pleasing flavor to the food served on them).

Because of its heft, the banana leaf can withstand greater heat than romaine or cabbage, which can also be used for wrapping and steaming, and they make for a presentation that is exponentially more appetizing than aluminum foil.

Banana leaves are sold cut and frozen through online vendors, or you can find them in your local Latin or Asian market. Bring some extra fresh fronds home and place them in a vase for a gorgeous tropical addition to your décor, or even use one long fresh leaf as a runner on your buffet table!

CHIPOTLE CREAM SHRIMP

1 cup all-purpose flour

4 tablespoons chopped fresh cilantro

Salt and freshly ground black pepper

2 pounds raw large shrimp (13 to 15 per pound), peeled but tails left intact, and deveined

6 tablespoons (¾ stick) unsalted butter

¼ cup dry white wine

1 cup heavy cream

2 tablespoons chopped canned chipotle chiles in adobo sauce

2 garlic cloves, minced

1½ tablespoons Worcestershire sauce

Serve this over rice, which will soak up the rich cream sauce. This dish is for the spicy-lover in you; if you want to prepare a milder version for guests or kids, you can use just the adobo sauce that accompanies the canned chipotles, and save the chiles for when you are preparing it for yourself. They'll last for months in a covered container in the fridge.

Put the flour in a shallow bowl. Add 3 tablespoons of the cilantro, 1 teaspoon salt, and 1 teaspoon pepper and toss to combine. Add the shrimp and toss to coat.

Melt the butter in a large heavy sauté pan over medium-high heat. Add the shrimp and sauté for 5 minutes, or until golden brown and just cooked through. Transfer the shrimp to a plate.

Add the wine to the same pan and boil for 2 minutes, or until slightly thickened. Add the cream, chipotles, garlic, and Worcestershire sauce to the pan and boil for 2 minutes, or until slightly reduced.

Return the shrimp to the pan and toss to coat them with the chipotle sauce. Season to taste with salt and pepper. Sprinkle with the remaining 1 tablespoon cilantro, and serve.

SALMON WITH A SWEET POTATO CRUST AND SMOKED SALMON–CHILE MULATO SAUCE

1 large sweet potato (about 10 ounces), peeled and shredded (about 2 cups)

1 large egg white, lightly beaten

Salt and freshly ground black pepper

¼ teaspoon ground nutmeg

Four 8-ounce center-cut skinless salmon fillets

2 tablespoons olive oil

Smoked Salmon–Chile Mulato Sauce (page 172)

The idea for this dish comes from a chef at culinary school who liked to bread salmon with shredded russet potatoes. Sweet potatoes add a whole new dimension to this delicate crust—a perfect counterpoint for the smoky sauce.

Mix the sweet potato, egg white, ½ teaspoon salt, ½ teaspoon black pepper, and the nutmeg in a medium bowl. Sprinkle the salmon all over with salt and pepper. Spoon one fourth of the sweet potato mixture over each salmon fillet, and pat it out to form a crust.

Heat the olive oil in a large heavy sauté pan over high heat. Carefully place the salmon pieces, crust side down, in the pan. Cook over medium-high heat for 4 minutes, or until the crust is golden brown. Using a spatula, carefully turn the salmon pieces over and cook for 8 minutes, or until the salmon is cooked through.

Spoon ¼ cup of the sauce onto each of 4 serving plates. Place a piece of salmon on each plate, and serve.

MUSSELS IN SAFFRON-CILANTRO CREAM

1½ cups heavy cream

1 teaspoon saffron threads, crushed

2 pounds mussels, scrubbed and debearded

¾ cup dry white wine

2 garlic cloves, minced

1 cup canned crushed tomatoes in puree

¼ cup plus 1 tablespoon chopped fresh cilantro

Salt and freshly ground black pepper

Even though saffron is a Spanish spice (and the world's most expensive one), it is often used in Mexican cuisine. I use it in this cream sauce for a richer, more flavorful alternative to the very popular mussels marinara. You can find bagged mussels, already scrubbed and debearded, at most markets. Be sure to discard any mussels with broken and open shells before you cook them, and any that don't open after they've been cooked.

Combine the cream and saffron in a medium saucepan, and bring to a boil. Lower the heat and simmer for 10 minutes, or until the cream thickens.

Combine the mussels, wine, and garlic in a large pot over medium-low heat. Cover and cook for 4 minutes, or until the mussels begin to open. Remove from the heat. Using a slotted spoon, transfer the mussels to a large bowl (discard any unopened mussels).

Add the saffron cream to the pot and stir in the tomatoes. Bring the sauce to a boil over high heat. Reduce the heat to medium and simmer for 5 minutes, or until the sauce thickens slightly.

Stir in the ¼ cup cilantro, and season the sauce to taste with salt and pepper. Pour the sauce over the mussels. Sprinkle them with the remaining 1 tablespoon cilantro, and serve.

VERACRUZ-STYLE SNAPPER

3 tablespoons olive oil

Four 6-ounce red snapper fillets

Salt and freshly ground black pepper

¾ cup chopped onion

4 garlic cloves, minced

1½ cups canned crushed tomatoes with juice

1 Anaheim chile, stemmed, seeded, and cut into thin strips

1 bay leaf

1 teaspoon crumbled dried oregano

½ cup halved pitted green olives

¼ cup capers, drained

Traditionally served with roasted small white potatoes (*papitas de cambray*) or white rice, this dish is a great representation of the European influence on the cuisine of the Gulf of Mexico. Add raisins and a pinch of cinnamon if you want some sweetness to contrast with the savory capers and olives; for a traditional take, garnish the fish with pickled jalapeños. Either way, a crisp white wine makes a lovely accompaniment.

Preheat the oven to 350°F.

Heat 1 tablespoon of the olive oil in a medium sauté pan over medium-high heat. Sprinkle the fish fillets on both sides with salt and pepper. Cook the fillets for 2 minutes per side, or until the fish is opaque and just cooked through. Transfer the fish fillets to a glass baking dish where they can fit snugly.

Heat the remaining 2 tablespoons olive oil in the same sauté pan over medium-high heat. Add the onion and garlic and cook for 5 minutes, or until the onion is translucent. Add the tomatoes, Anaheim chile, bay leaf, and oregano and bring to a boil. Reduce the heat to medium, cover, and simmer the sauce for 6 minutes, or until the chiles soften. Uncover the pan, add the olives and capers, and cook for 4 minutes, or until the flavors combine. Season the sauce to taste with salt and pepper.

Pour the sauce over the fish in the baking dish. Transfer the dish to the oven and bake for 5 minutes, or until heated through. Remove the bay leaf. Serve the fillets topped with the sauce.

SHRIMP-STUFFED NOPALES

2 tablespoons olive oil

1 cup chopped red bell pepper

1 cup chopped onion

1 cup chopped seeded tomato

1 pound raw shrimp, peeled, deveined, and chopped

Salt and freshly ground black pepper

4 cleaned prickly pear cactus paddles (1¼ pounds)

Lime wedges, for serving

Bottled hot sauce (such as Huichol), for serving

Nopales are cactus paddles. They may be hard to come by if you don't live in a border state or have access to a Mexican market. If you're lucky, you'll find prickly pear cactus paddles, which are packed with soluble fiber, vitamins, and minerals and reduce the glycemic effect of a meal. The stuffing is the star of this recipe, so if nopales are nowhere in sight, you can use corn tortillas for equally delicious (although not as pretty) results. At my house, we grill plain nopales until they are tender and a little charred and serve them with some lime wedges.

Heat the olive oil in a medium-size heavy saucepan over medium-high heat. Add the bell pepper, onion, and tomato and sauté for 8 minutes, or until the pepper is nearly tender. Add the shrimp and sauté for 2 minutes, or until just cooked through. Season the stuffing to taste with salt and pepper, and set it aside.

Heat a grill pan over medium-high heat. Using a small sharp knife, carefully cut a slit along one long side of each nopal without cutting all the way through, to make something resembling a pita pocket. Grill the nopales for 4 minutes per side, or until they are tender and grill marks appear.

Stuff the nopales with the shrimp mixture, dividing it equally, and serve with lime wedges and hot sauce.

SARANDEADO-STYLE BUTTERFLIED WHOLE FISH

4 tablespoons (½ stick) cold unsalted butter, cubed

1 whole porgy, gutted with head and tail intact

Salt and freshly ground black pepper

1 tablespoon garlic powder

1 teaspoon bottled hot sauce (such as Huichol)

2 limes, halved, plus lime wedges for serving

½ orange

Six 6-inch corn tortillas, warmed (see page 59)

Sarandeado, as a technique, refers to grilling a cleaned fish in a basket, constantly flipping it from one side to the other in order to preserve all the juices and flavors before they seep out of the fish. In this recipe we use the oven, so there's no need for a fish basket or even a grill. It is essential, however, that you use a properly butterflied fish (the skin prevents the juices from seeping out and yields a moist and succulent fish). I strongly suggest asking your fishmonger to do it for you.

Preheat the oven to 350°F.

Line a large baking sheet with foil and dot it with half of the butter.

Butterfly the fish by cutting it almost in half horizontally and opening it like a book. Carefully cut out and remove the spine.

Place the fish, skin side down, on the foil-lined baking sheet. Roll up the edges of the foil to come close to the edge of the fish, to create a rim that will prevent the juices from spilling onto the baking sheet. Sprinkle the fish with salt and pepper, then with the garlic powder. Drizzle the hot sauce over the fish, and then squeeze the limes over it. Squeeze the orange half all over the fish. Then, using the flesh side of the orange, brush the fish all over to form a wet paste on top of the fish. Dot the fish with the remaining butter.

Bake the fish for 15 minutes, or until just cooked through. Turn on the broiler and broil the fish for 8 to 10 minutes, or until browned. Serve with warm tortillas to make tacos, and lime wedges for squeezing over the fish.

BAKED COD WITH ANCHOVIES AND LIME

Two 6-ounce cod fillets, pinbones removed

Salt and freshly ground black pepper

6 very thin lime slices, plus lime wedges for serving

8 anchovy fillets, thinly sliced lengthwise

2 tablespoons chopped pitted kalamata olives

2 tablespoons minced drained capers

2 teaspoons chopped fresh rosemary

2 tablespoons olive oil

This is a light, healthful Mediterranean-inspired dish that is super-easy to make and can be on the table in 20 minutes—great for a weeknight dinner for two. If you have a crowd (or a big family like mine), go ahead and adjust the recipe accordingly. A note about anchovies, which I think get a bad rap: They are actually a wonderful way to add salt to a dish or sauce and are very popular in some Baja dishes (like the world-renowned Caesar Salad). Fresh anchovies have a gentler flavor than those packaged in a tin, but either will work here.

Preheat the oven to 425°F.

Place the cod fillets in a glass baking dish and sprinkle with salt and pepper. Top each fillet with 3 lime slices and then with the anchovies, dividing them equally. Sprinkle the fillets with the olives, capers, and rosemary. Drizzle with the olive oil.

Bake for 18 minutes, or until the fish is cooked through. Serve with lime wedges.

MY FISH TACOS

LEMON CREAM

⅓ cup mayonnaise

⅓ cup sour cream

⅓ cup Mexican *crema* (see page 70) or additional sour cream

1 teaspoon grated lemon zest

2 tablespoons fresh lemon juice

Salt and freshly ground black pepper

FISH

Oil, for frying

1 cup all-purpose flour

Salt and freshly ground black pepper

2 pounds skinless halibut fillet, cut into 5 x ½-inch strips

Beer Batter (page 50)

Twelve to sixteen 6-inch corn tortillas, warmed (see page 59)

2 cups shredded cabbage

Fresh Tomatillo-Avocado Salsa (page 183)

Canned pickled jalapeño chiles (optional)

I have eaten more than my share of fish tacos while living in Baja. But the beach is a half-hour drive from my house, so I was on a mission to find a fish taco recipe that I could make at home—one that was as delicious and authentic as the taco they serve at my favorite Rosarito taco shack. This is what I came up with—and I'm happy to say it competes!

To make the lemon cream, whisk the mayonnaise, sour cream, and *crema* in a medium bowl. Whisk in the lemon zest, lemon juice, and 2 tablespoons water. Season the cream sauce to taste with salt and pepper. (The sauce can be made 3 days ahead. Cover and refrigerate.)

To cook the fish, add enough oil to a large skillet to reach a depth of 1 inch. Heat the oil to 350°F.

Combine the flour and 1 teaspoon salt on a plate and mix to combine. Sprinkle the fish pieces all over with salt and pepper, and then coat them with the prepared flour.

Working in batches, turn the floured fish pieces in the beer batter, coating them on both sides. Fry in the hot oil for 5 minutes, or until the fish is golden brown and cooked through. Transfer to paper towels to drain.

Make tacos with the tortillas and fish, topping each with some of the lemon cream, shredded cabbage, tomatillo salsa, and pickled jalapeños if desired.

MICHELADAS AND SPICY SEAFOOD ARE THE COMMON REMEDY FOR A BAD HANGOVER. TO MAKE A *MICHELADA*, FREEZE A BEER MUG; THEN MOISTEN THE RIM WITH LIME JUICE AND COAT IT WITH SALT. ADD ICE AND ¼ CUP FRESH LIME JUICE (SOMEONE ACTUALLY MADE ME ONE OF THESE WITH FAKE LIME JUICE ONCE—ONLY ONCE). ADD BEER, AND DRINK BEFORE THE ICE MELTS.

AUNT LAURA'S TUNA-STUFFED CHILES

¾ cup sliced carrot

Two 6-ounce cans albacore tuna in water, drained

3 tablespoons mayonnaise

1 cup fresh peas (from 1 pound in the shell)

½ cup fresh corn kernels (from 1 ear)

Salt and freshly ground black pepper

⅔ cup olive oil

2 small red onions, thinly sliced

2 garlic cloves

⅔ cup distilled white vinegar

2 bay leaves

2 teaspoons crumbled dried oregano

8 Anaheim chiles, charred (see page 35), peeled, stemmed, and seeded, left whole for stuffing

Yes, I use canned tuna for this dish—and you will love it. I generally prefer fresh ingredients over packaged items, but these stuffed peppers are worth breaking the rule. The mild flavor of the canned albacore allows the flavor of the pickled onions to shine through. My aunt Laura, who passed this recipe on to me, makes it with canned chiles (they are available in Mexico already charred, peeled, and ready to stuff). But for me, half of this dish's success is the exquisite smell of the chiles charring on the burner. You can't buy anticipation in a can.

Bring a saucepan of salted water to a boil. Add the carrot slices and cook until just crisp-tender, about 3 minutes. Drain, and set them aside to cool.

Combine the tuna, mayonnaise, peas, and corn in a small bowl. Season to taste with salt and pepper and set aside.

Heat the oil in a large saucepan over medium heat. When the oil is hot, add the onions and garlic and cook for 5 minutes, or until the onions are slightly cooked but still crisp. Add ⅔ cup water and the vinegar, and bring to a simmer. Add the carrots, bay leaves, and oregano. Simmer for 8 minutes, or until the vegetables are crisp-tender and almost all of the vinegar has evaporated.

Stuff the chiles with the tuna mixture, and fit them snugly into a 9 x 13-inch glass baking dish. Pour the warm pickled mixture over the stuffed chiles, and allow to cool to room temperature. Cover and chill for 2 hours or overnight. Serve cold.

JALAPEÑO ROAST CHICKEN WITH BABY BROCCOLI

½ cup (packed) fresh oregano leaves

1 shallot

4 garlic cloves

4 tablespoons (½ stick) unsalted butter

3 tablespoons olive oil

1 jalapeño chile, stemmed and seeded

Salt and freshly ground black pepper

One 5½-pound whole roasting chicken

1½ cups chicken broth, or more if needed

¾ cup dry white wine

2 pounds baby broccoli (see Tip)

There was always a roast chicken in our fridge when I was growing up—but I'd be lying if I said my mom cooked it. There was a wonderful rotisserie place a few blocks from my house and they would deliver a succulent roast chicken, fresh salsa, homemade tortillas, and *frijoles charros* (like the frijoles on page 155 but with tons of bacon in the mix). We'd all stand around the kitchen table and make soft tacos, adding a few slices of avocado. We used leftovers for chicken salad, *flautas* (rolled up and fried chicken tacos), or *tostadas* (fried tortillas spread with refried beans, topped with shredded chicken, shredded iceberg lettuce, *crema,* salsa, avocado slices, and, in my house, a drizzle of olive oil and red wine vinegar).

This recipe is so easy and yields such a flavorful, succulent chicken that I doubt any rotisserie place in your neighborhood can rival it. And I doubt you'll have leftovers. But if you do, go to town with tortillas, beans, avocado, and any of the salsas in this book and make tacos.

Position a rack in the center of the oven and preheat the oven to 400°F.

Combine the oregano, shallot, garlic, butter, 2 tablespoons of the olive oil, the jalapeño, 1 teaspoon salt, and ½ teaspoon pepper in a food processor, and process to form a coarse paste.

Pat the chicken dry and then place it, breast side up, on a rack in a large roasting pan. Using your fingers, loosen the skin from the chicken breast, legs, and thighs without detaching it. Spread half of the jalapeño paste under the skin. Tie the chicken legs together with kitchen string. Spread the remaining jalapeño paste all over the outside of the chicken.

Pour the chicken broth and wine into the roasting pan. Roast the chicken for 1 hour, basting with the pan juices every 20 minutes and adding more broth to the pan if it's beginning to dry out.

Remove the roasting pan from the oven. Arrange the baby broccoli snugly around the chicken on the rack. Drizzle the remaining 1 tablespoon olive oil over the broccoli, and sprinkle with salt and pepper. Roast the chicken with the baby broccoli, basting occasionally with the pan juices, until a meat thermometer inserted into the innermost part of the thigh (but not touching the bone) registers 160°F, about 30 minutes.

Place the chicken on a platter, surround it with the baby broccoli, and serve.

TIP BABY BROCCOLI IS ALSO KNOWN AS BROCCOLINI. DON'T CONFUSE IT WITH BROCCOLI RABE, WHICH HAS A BITTER TASTE. IF YOU CAN'T FIND BABY BROCCOLI, USE 2 POUNDS REGULAR BROCCOLI HEADS; QUARTER THEM BY SLICING THROUGH THE STEM AND FLORETS SO THAT EACH QUARTER HAS SOME STEM ATTACHED.

CILANTRO TANDOORI CHICKEN WITH GRILLED PINEAPPLE SALSA

1½ cups plain yogurt

1 cup (packed) fresh cilantro leaves

4 garlic cloves

One ½-inch-thick piece fresh ginger, peeled

1½ teaspoons ground cumin

1½ teaspoons ground coriander

1 teaspoon salt

One 4-pound chicken, cut into 6 pieces (2 breasts, 2 thighs, 2 legs)

Grilled Pineapple Salsa (page 173)

I love tandoori-style cooking, derived from India's clay *tandoor* oven, because the chicken stays unbelievably moist and juicy, even after grilling. To give new life to the traditional yogurt-based marinade, I add flavors more indigenous to Mexico and pair this dish with a pineapple and serrano salsa.

Combine the yogurt, cilantro, garlic, ginger, cumin, coriander, and salt in a food processor or blender, and blend until smooth. Transfer the marinade to a large bowl. Add the chicken pieces and turn to coat. Cover, and refrigerate overnight.

Prepare a grill to medium-high heat, or heat a grill pan over medium-high heat.

Remove the chicken from the marinade, shaking off the excess. Discard the marinade. Grill the chicken for 12 minutes per side, or until just cooked through. Transfer the chicken to a platter, top with the salsa, and serve.

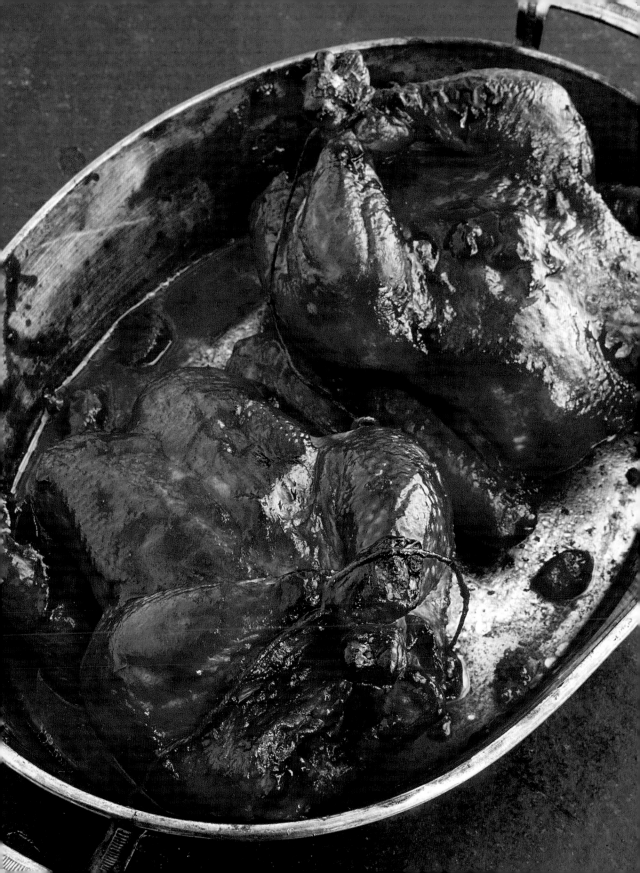

GAME HENS IN APRICOT, TEQUILA, AND CALIFORNIA CHILE SAUCE

3 cups chicken broth, or more as needed

2 tablespoons unsalted butter, melted

4 tablespoons golden tequila

Two 2-pound Cornish game hens, thawed if frozen

3 California chiles, stemmed and seeded

½ cup apricot preserves

Salt and freshly ground black pepper

Fresh apricot halves, for garnish

This recipe is one of my favorites ever. It comes from my aunt Marcela, a chef who inspired me to enter the magical world of the culinary arts. We not only share the same name and the same career, we also agree that sweet and spicy is one of the best combinations when preparing Mexican food.

Store-bought apricot preserves, used here, work well; just be sure to buy the best you can find. A kitchen syringe is a useful tool for injecting the hens with a flavorful mixture of broth, butter, and tequila. The result is a moist and succulent dish.

Preheat the oven to 350°F.

Mix ½ cup of the chicken broth, the melted butter, and 2 tablespoons of the tequila in a small glass bowl. Using a kitchen syringe, inject the mixture all over the hens, about ½ inch deep into the flesh. (If the butter in the mixture solidifies, warm it in a microwave.)

Put the chiles and 2 cups of the broth in a small saucepan, and bring to a boil over high heat. Remove the pan from the heat. Let stand for 5 minutes to soften the chiles. Then transfer the mixture to a blender and puree until smooth. Strain the chile mixture into a small bowl, pressing on the sieve to extract as much liquid as possible. Discard whatever is left in the sieve.

RECIPE CONTINUES

Mix ¼ cup of the preserves and ¼ cup of the chile mixture in a medium bowl. Season heavily with salt and pepper. Rub the mixture all over the hens, working some of it between the skin and the breast. Put the hens on a rack in a large roasting pan. Add the remaining ½ cup broth to the roasting pan.

Roast, basting with the pan drippings every 20 minutes, for 1 hour, or until a thermometer inserted into a thigh registers 160°F. Add more broth if the juices begin to dry out.

Transfer the hens to a platter. Strain the pan juices into a medium saucepan. Add the remaining 2 tablespoons tequila, ¼ cup apricot preserves, and chile mixture. Bring to a boil over high heat. Reduce the heat and simmer for 5 minutes, or until the sauce thickens slightly. Season with salt and pepper to taste. Pour the sauce over the hens, garnish the platter with fresh apricot halves, and serve.

MEXICAN CHILE-LIME POWDER

Mexican chile-lime powder is part of our candy culture; you can find it at every kid's party, along with a piñata. My favorite brands are Miguelito, Tajin, and Lucas. Most of them are a combination of powdered chiles, dehydrated lime, salt, and sometimes a little sugar—and they should definitely not be confused with the ground chiles found in the spice section of your supermarket. The powder is shaken onto mangoes, watermelon, halved oranges, jícama, cucumber—any fresh fruit or vegetable, really—to snack on. It's a sure way to get my son Fausto to eat his sliced apples. It is also great on grilled corn, popcorn, and frozen fruit bars.

When I was a kid I used to dip almost everything into Lucas or even lick it off my hand. Now as an adult, I use it to coat the rim of a cocktail glass or an ice-cold beer mug.

EASY CHICKEN MOLE

CHICKEN

One 3½-pound whole chicken

2 onions, quartered

2 carrots, chopped

2 celery stalks, chopped

4 garlic cloves

2 bay leaves

MOLE SAUCE

5 pasilla chiles, stemmed and seeded

2 tablespoons olive oil

2 cups chopped onion

2 garlic cloves, minced

3 tablespoons smooth peanut butter

2 corn tostadas (see page 23), grilled and torn into pieces

1 tablespoon sugar

1 teaspoon crumbled dried oregano

5.5 ounces Ibarra chocolate (see page 117), chopped

Salt and freshly ground black pepper

I'm a little obsessed with mole (Mexico's national dish, also known as *mole poblano*). I even visited its birthplace, the Convent of Santa Rosa in the beautiful colonial city of Puebla. Traditional mole takes days to make and is just as marvelous and multileveled as the most complex French sauce. Here you get a much easier version with nearly authentic results in terms of flavor. Do a little experiment and taste your mole right before you add the chocolate and then right after you add it. If you don't get what it means when gourmands talk about "depth of flavor," you'll get it when you make this comparison. My great-grandmother, grandmother, mother, and I all like to sprinkle it with plenty of additional sugar and a dollop of sour cream after it's on the plate. You can make the sauce on its own and use it for very impressive enchiladas—or do as I did when I was a kid: spoon a few tablespoons over Mexican rice and chow down.

To cook the chicken, combine the chicken, onions, carrots, celery, garlic, and bay leaves in a large heavy pot. Add 12 cups water and bring to a boil over high heat. Reduce the heat to medium and simmer until the chicken is cooked through, about 45 minutes. Transfer the chicken to a large bowl, and let it cool. Cut the chicken into 6 pieces and set aside in the refrigerator.

Strain the cooking liquid into a large saucepan (discard the vegetables) and boil over high heat until reduced to 3 cups, about 1 hour. Remove from the heat.

RECIPE CONTINUES

To make the mole sauce, measure out and rewarm (if necessary) 1¼ cups of the reduced cooking liquid. Soak the chiles in the liquid for 15 minutes. Drain well, and discard the chile-soaking liquid.

Heat the olive oil in a large heavy saucepan over medium heat. Add the onion and garlic and sauté for 5 minutes, or until translucent. Transfer the mixture to a blender and add the chiles, 1½ cups reduced cooking liquid, and the peanut butter, tostadas, sugar, and oregano. Blend until very smooth. Transfer the sauce to a saucepan and bring to a boil over high heat. Reduce the heat to medium, cover, and simmer for 20 minutes.

Stir the chocolate into the mole, and season to taste with salt and pepper. Add the cooked chicken pieces and stir until the chicken is heated through, about 5 minutes.

IBARRA CHOCOLATE

Flavored with cinnamon, almonds, and vanilla, Ibarra chocolate is available in Mexican markets and some supermarkets. Mexican chocolate has a much grainier texture than other chocolates. It's used in the preparation of a Mexican hot chocolate drink and certain specialties such as Ancho-Chocolate Braised Short Ribs (page 128). One ounce of semisweet chocolate, ½ teaspoon ground cinnamon, and 1 drop almond extract can be substituted for 1 ounce Mexican chocolate.

SURF AND TURF MOLCAJETE

1 boneless skinless chicken breast half

4 ounces flank steak

8 raw jumbo shrimp, peeled but tails left intact, and deveined

Salt and black pepper

6 scallions

3 tablespoons olive oil

¼ onion

1½ whole tomatoes

2 garlic cloves

2 California chiles, stemmed, seeded, and torn into pieces

2 ancho chiles, stemmed, seeded, and torn into pieces

2 dried árbol chiles, stemmed, seeded, and cut into pieces

1 tablespoon crumbled dried oregano

1 tablespoon cumin seeds

1 teaspoon tomato bouillon

2 slices panela cheese

Six to eight 6-inch corn tortillas, warmed (see page 59)

This is a simple dish with an impressive presentation, and it works with any combination of grilled meat, fish, poultry, or vegetables. A *molcajete* is a mortar made of lava rock that is usually used with a pestle (also made of lava rock) to make fresh salsas. Because it is made with a natural rock, it has an excellent ability to preserve heat and keep a dish hot, and that's how I use it in this recipe. If you do not have two molcajetes, ovenproof earthenware bowls (about the size of cereal bowls) are an acceptable substitute.

Prepare a grill or grill pan to medium-high heat.

Sprinkle the chicken, flank steak, and shrimp with salt and pepper. Grill the chicken until cooked through, about 6 minutes per side. Transfer the chicken to a platter and cover with aluminum foil to keep warm.

Grill the flank steak to the desired doneness, about 5 minutes per side for medium. Add it to the platter.

Grill the shrimp until just cooked through, about 3 minutes per side. Add them to the platter.

Grill the scallions until brown, about 3 minutes per side. Add them to the platter.

Heat 2 tablespoons of the oil in a large heavy saucepan over medium-high heat. Add the onion, tomatoes, and garlic and cook for 8 minutes, or until the onion is golden. Add all three kinds of chiles, the oregano, cumin, and bouillon, and stir for 2 minutes, or until fragrant. Add 1 cup water to the saucepan

RECIPE CONTINUES

and bring to boil. Reduce the heat to medium-low and simmer for 2 minutes, or until the chiles are soft. Let the mixture cool slightly. Transfer the mixture to a blender, add 1 cup water, and blend until smooth. Strain the sauce into a medium bowl.

Heat the remaining 1 tablespoon oil in the same saucepan over medium heat. Return the sauce to the pan and simmer for 2 minutes, or until slightly thickened. Season the sauce to taste with salt and pepper. (The sauce can be made 1 day ahead. Cool, cover, and refrigerate. Bring to a boil before continuing.)

Preheat the oven to 350°F.

Place 2 molcajetes in the oven and heat them for 10 minutes. Using oven mitts, remove them from the oven and transfer them to a heatproof surface (be careful, as the molcajetes get extremely hot).

Cut the chicken and flank steak into ¾-inch-wide strips. Arrange the grilled chicken and steak strips, shrimp, scallions, and cheese slices around the edges of the molcajetes. Pour the boiling sauce into the center. Serve very hot, with tortillas to make tacos.

CHORIZO QUICHE

Nonstick cooking spray

1½ cups all-purpose flour, plus more for rolling

¼ teaspoon salt

8 tablespoons (1 stick) cold unsalted butter, cubed

6 ounces raw chorizo, casing removed

5 large eggs

½ cup whole milk

½ cup heavy cream

1½ cups grated Emmenthal cheese (about 6 ounces)

1 cup diced boiled potato

This is my interpretation of the traditional Mexican dish of sautéed chorizo and boiled potatoes, which is usually eaten with tacos or *queso fundido* (melted cheese fondue). In Mexico, chorizo, potatoes, and cheese always go together. But my favorite part of this dish is the crust—it's perfect for any quiche.

Spray a 9-inch glass pie dish with nonstick cooking spray.

Mix the flour and salt in a food processor. Add the butter and pulse to form a coarse meal. With the motor running, add 6 tablespoons cold water in a slow stream, processing until the dough comes together. Then gather the dough into a ball and transfer it to a floured surface. Roll the dough out to form a 12-inch round. Transfer the dough to the prepared pie dish. Crimp the edges between your fingers to make a decorative border, removing any excess dough. Freeze the crust for 20 minutes.

Preheat the oven to 425°F.

Line the crust with foil and fill it with pie weights or uncooked dried beans. Bake for 15 minutes. Then remove the foil and beans and continue to bake for 5 minutes, or until the crust is golden brown. Let the crust cool completely. (The crust can be made 1 day ahead. Cover and store at room temperature.) Leave the oven on.

RECIPE CONTINUES

Cook the chorizo in a dry medium-size heavy sauté pan over medium heat for 8 minutes, or until dry and crisp. Let the chorizo cool on a paper towel–lined plate.

Whisk the eggs, milk, and cream in a large bowl. Mix in the chorizo, cheese, and potato. Pour the mixture into the cooled crust. Bake for 35 minutes, or until the filling is puffed and a knife inserted into the center comes out clean. Serve hot or at room temperature, cut into wedges.

TIP MAKING ANY TYPE OF CRUST INTIMIDATES SOME PEOPLE IN THE KITCHEN, ESPECIALLY BEGINNERS. WHEN IT COMES TO BAKING, I STRONGLY SUGGEST FOLLOWING RECIPES EXACTLY—MAKING SURE THE BUTTER IS COLD (FREEZE IT AFTER YOU'VE CUBED IT TO ENSURE IT'S AT ITS COLDEST) RESULTS IN A FLAKIER CRUST, FOR EXAMPLE, AS DOES TAKING CARE NOT TO OVERWORK THE DOUGH WHEN GATHERING IT TOGETHER. IF YOU STILL FIND MAKING A CRUST IS NOT YOUR THING— OR YOU SIMPLY DON'T HAVE TIME—REST ASSURED THAT THE CHORIZO FILLING IS DELICIOUS IN A STORE-BOUGHT PIE CRUST, TOO. YOU CAN BUY READYMADE DOUGH, ROLL IT OUT YOURSELF, AND FOLLOW THE SAME DIRECTIONS, OR EVEN EASIER, PURCHASE A PREFORMED FROZEN CRUST. THAW AND BAKE THE CRUST ON ITS OWN UNTIL LIGHT GOLDEN BROWN ACCORDING TO PACKAGE DIRECTIONS. ONCE COOL, ADD THE FILLING AND FOLLOW THE RECIPE INSTRUCTIONS FOR BAKING.

ROASTED PORK LOIN WITH PINEAPPLE GLAZE

BRINE

½ cup kosher salt

½ cup (packed) light brown sugar

1 tablespoon black peppercorns

1 tablespoon coriander seeds

4 bay leaves

When it comes to pork loins, I am very much in favor of brining. You do have to start a day ahead, but the end result is succulent and juicy.

To brine the pork, combine the salt, brown sugar, peppercorns, coriander seeds, bay leaves, and 2 cups warm water in a large bowl. Stir until the salt dissolves. Add 6 cups cold water. Add the pork (the pork should be submerged in the liquid), cover, and refrigerate overnight.

To cook the pork, preheat the oven to 400°F.

Mix the garlic, the 2 tablespoons olive oil, and the salt, pepper, thyme, and rosemary in a small bowl. Remove the pork from the brine and pat it dry (discard the brine). Spread the herb mixture over the side of the roast that is not covered with fat.

Heat the remaining ½ teaspoon olive oil in a medium-size heavy sauté pan over high heat. Add the pork, fat side down, and sear for 4 minutes, or until browned. Carefully turn the pork over onto the herb-coated side and sear for another 4 minutes, or until browned. Transfer the pork loin to a 10 x 7 x 2-inch glass baking dish (or any dish where it fits leaving a 1-inch

PORK

1 center-cut boneless pork loin roast (about 3½ pounds)

5 garlic cloves, minced

2 tablespoons plus ½ teaspoon olive oil

1 tablespoon salt

½ teaspoon freshly ground black pepper

2 teaspoons chopped fresh thyme

2 teaspoons chopped fresh rosemary

⅓ cup dry white wine

1 cup pineapple juice

1 pound pearl onions, peeled

border). Add the wine to the same sauté pan you used to sear the pork, and cook, scraping the bottom of the pan to remove the browned bits, for 1 minute, or until almost evaporated. Stir in the pineapple juice and remove from the heat. Pour the mixture over the pork and arrange the pearl onions around the roast.

Roast the pork, basting with the pan juices every 20 minutes, until a thermometer inserted into the center registers 150°F, about 1 hour and 40 minutes. Transfer the pork to a cutting board, tent it with foil, and let it stand for 10 minutes. Then cut the pork into ¼- to ½-inch-thick slices, and top them with the pearl onions and sauce.

COCHINITA PIBIL
PORK RUBBED IN ACHIOTE AND ORANGE JUICE AND BAKED IN BANANA LEAVES

2 tablespoons annatto paste (see opposite)

½ cup fresh lime juice

1½ cups fresh orange juice

¼ teaspoon crumbled dried oregano

2 garlic cloves, minced

2 teaspoons salt

4 pounds pork butt, cut into 2-inch pieces

Two 4- to 5-foot-long banana leaves (see page 95), plus more for garnish (optional)

8 tablespoons (1 stick) unsalted butter, melted

Twelve to sixteen 6-inch corn tortillas

Pickled Onions (page 186)

The thing I love the most about Mexico is that everything has a story. In this recipe the word *pibil* comes from a Mayan word for stone-lined pits, used for cooking underground. Today *pibil* refers to the technique of steaming meat in a sealed dish in the oven. In the Yucatán, where this dish comes from, it is prepared with Seville oranges, which are tart and bitter. These oranges aren't readily available in other areas, including Baja, so here we add lime juice to give that distinctive kick.

Mix the annatto paste, lime juice, orange juice, oregano, garlic, and salt in a large bowl to form a paste. Add the pork and toss to coat. Cover, and marinate in the refrigerator for at least 4 hours or overnight.

Preheat the oven to 325°F.

Turn on a gas burner to medium-high heat. Working with one at a time, very slowly pass an entire banana leaf directly over the gas flame until the leaf is opaque and pliable. Crisscross the banana leaves in the bottom of a Dutch oven or other large heavy pot (they'll hang over the edges). Put the pork, with all of the paste, inside the pot. Pour the melted butter over the pork. Wrap the banana leaves over the top and moisten the leaves with a few tablespoons of water (to avoid burning). Cover the pot with aluminum foil and then with its own lid. Bake for 2½ hours, or until the pork is very tender and falling apart.

Make tacos using the tortillas, pork, and pickled onions. Set them on a platter garnished with additional pieces of banana leaves, if desired.

ANNATTO
PASTE

I use annatto paste for everything from making marinades and flavoring butter to coloring rice. It is also used to color cheese, margarine, and smoked fish. This musky product of the annatto tree (called *achiote* in its seed form) is available in Latin American, Spanish, and East Indian markets.

ANCHO-CHOCOLATE BRAISED SHORT RIBS

5 pounds 2- to 3-inch beef short ribs, on the bone (see Tip)

2 onions, quartered

10 garlic cloves, smashed with the side of a knife

1 bay leaf

1 tablespoon black peppercorns

Salt

2 tomatoes

1 head garlic, wrapped in aluminum foil

4 tablespoons olive oil

Freshly ground black pepper

15 ancho chiles, stemmed, seeded, and torn into pieces

1 teaspoon ground cumin

2 teaspoons crumbled dried oregano

2 ounces Ibarra chocolate (see page 117; ⅔ of a 3.1-ounce disk)

Chocolate and chiles have been paired up for centuries in Mexico. Ancho-infused hot chocolate was a drink reserved for royalty, believed to produce strength and virility. The combo is especially tasty with beefy short ribs. You can substitute bittersweet chocolate for the Mexican chocolate; just add a pinch each of sugar and cinnamon and a few drops of almond extract—the ingredients that make Mexican chocolate unique.

Combine the short ribs, one of the onions, the garlic cloves, bay leaf, peppercorns, and 1 tablespoon salt in a large heavy pot. Add water to cover, and bring to a boil over high heat. Reduce the heat to medium-low and simmer, uncovered, for 1½ hours, or until the meat is cooked through.

Meanwhile, preheat the oven to 400°F.

Arrange the remaining onion, the tomatoes, and the head of garlic on a large baking sheet. Drizzle the onion and tomatoes with 2 tablespoons of the olive oil, and sprinkle generously with salt and pepper. Roast for 1 hour, or until the vegetables are tender and browning in spots and the head of garlic is tender when pierced. Allow to cool slightly. Then transfer the tomatoes and onion to a blender. Squeeze the garlic cloves from their papery skin into the blender, and blend until smooth. Transfer the tomato puree to a medium bowl and set it aside.

RECIPE CONTINUES

TIP SHORT RIBS CAN BE PURCHASED ON THE BONE OR BONELESS. I PREFER THE BONE-IN PIECES BECAUSE YOU GET SO MUCH FLAVOR WHEN YOU COOK MEAT ON THE BONE, ESPECIALLY IN BRAISED DISHES SUCH AS THIS ONE.

When the short ribs are cooked through, strain them, reserving the meat and cooking liquid separately; discard all the vegetables and seasonings.

Put the ancho chiles in a medium bowl and cover with 3 cups of the warm reserved cooking liquid. Let stand for 15 minutes, or until the chiles are soft. Transfer the chiles and liquid to the blender and puree to a paste. (There is no need to clean the blender since everything is for the same sauce.)

Heat the remaining 2 tablespoons olive oil in a large heavy pot over medium-high heat. Add the ancho paste and simmer for 3 minutes. Add the tomato puree and 3 cups of the reserved cooking liquid. Stir in the cumin and oregano, and then the cooked short ribs. Bring the sauce to a boil. Reduce the heat to medium and simmer, uncovered, for 1¾ hours, or until the meat is very tender (adding more reserved cooking liquid if the sauce is too dry).

Stir in the chocolate until melted. Season the sauce to taste with salt and pepper. Spoon the meat and sauce into shallow bowls, and serve.

SALPICÓN
COLD SHREDDED BEEF SALAD

2 pounds boneless beef brisket

1 large onion, quartered

Salt

¾ cup olive oil

6 tablespoons distilled white vinegar

¼ cup fresh lime juice

¼ cup minced red onion

2 tablespoons crumbled dried oregano

Freshly ground black pepper

1 cup chopped seeded tomato

1 cup chopped seeded peeled cucumber

½ cup capers, drained

¼ cup chopped fresh cilantro

4 radishes, finely chopped

24 tostadas (see Tips, page 23)

3 avocados, halved, pitted, peeled, and sliced

Bottled hot sauce (such as Huichol)

This shredded beef salad is perfect for a crowd or for a leftover-friendly family. It actually tastes better a day or two after you make it, when the flavors have had more time to combine. Although capers aren't traditionally found in salpicón, I think they make perfect sense in this summer dish, adding just a touch of salt.

Put the brisket in a large pot and add enough water to cover the meat by 1 inch. Add the onion pieces and ¼ cup salt. Bring to a boil. Then reduce the heat to medium and simmer, partially covered, for 2½ hours, or until the brisket is very tender. (Add more water if needed to keep the meat covered.) Remove the pot from the heat and let the brisket cool to room temperature in the cooking liquid. Then drain the brisket, discard the water, and cover tightly with plastic wrap. Refrigerate the brisket. (Brisket can be made 1 day ahead.)

Meanwhile, prepare the vinaigrette by whisking the olive oil, vinegar, lime juice, red onion, and oregano in a medium bowl. Season the vinaigrette with salt and pepper.

Shred the cooled brisket into a large bowl. Add the tomato, cucumber, capers, cilantro, and radishes, and toss to combine. Add the vinaigrette and toss to coat. Season the salpicón with additional salt and pepper if needed. Spoon enough salpicón on a tostada to cover and then garnish with avocado slices. Serve with hot sauce.

OSSO BUCO DON TONY

2 veal shanks (about 2 pounds total)

Salt and freshly ground black pepper

½ cup all-purpose flour

3 tablespoons olive oil

1 cup chopped onion

½ cup chopped carrot

½ cup chopped celery

2 ancho chiles, stemmed, seeded, and torn into pieces

4 garlic cloves: 2 minced, 2 whole

1 cup dry white wine

One 14.5-ounce can peeled tomatoes, with juice

½ cup beef broth

4 tablespoons grated lime zest (from 6 to 8 limes)

⅓ cup (packed) fresh cilantro leaves

My dad, Antonio (a.k.a. Tony), inspired this dish. Like a painter's body of work, his culinary life is marked by distinct periods. When he went through an osso buco period, I decided that if I was going to be making a lot of osso buco, it was going to be a Mexican osso buco, spiked with lime, chiles, cilantro, and garlic.

Preheat the oven to 350°F.

Season the veal shanks all over with salt and pepper. Place the flour on a plate and dredge the veal shanks in the flour, shaking off the excess.

Heat the olive oil in a large heavy ovenproof pot over medium-high heat. Add the veal shanks and cook for 5 minutes per side, or until browned all over. Transfer them to a plate.

Add the onion, carrot, celery, chiles, and minced garlic to the same pot. Cook for 3 minutes, or until the vegetables begin to brown. Add the wine and bring to a boil, scraping up the browned bits. Cook for 2 minutes, or until slightly reduced. Then stir in the canned tomatoes with juice, beef broth, and 3 tablespoons of the lime zest.

Return the veal shanks to the pot and push them down into the sauce. Bring the sauce to a boil and then turn off the heat. Cover the pot tightly, and carefully transfer it to the oven. Braise the veal shanks for 2 hours, or until tender.

Uncover the pot and continue to cook in the oven for 25 minutes, or until the sauce thickens. Meanwhile, combine the cilantro, whole garlic cloves, and remaining 1 tablespoon lime zest in a food processor and pulse 5 or 6 times, or until finely chopped.

Transfer the veal shanks to a platter. Season the sauce to taste with salt and pepper, and pour it over the veal shanks. Sprinkle the cilantro mixture generously over the osso buco, and serve.

RACK OF LAMB WITH ANCHO CRUST

1 ancho chile, stemmed and seeded

4 tablespoons (½ stick) unsalted butter

3 large shallots, minced

2 teaspoons chopped fresh thyme

1½ cups fresh bread crumbs made from French bread

Salt and freshly ground black pepper

1 tablespoon olive oil

2 well-trimmed racks of lamb (each about 1¼ pounds)

3 teaspoons Dijon mustard

Jalapeño jelly (optional)

An ancho chile is a dried poblano, perfect for adding a little heat to this bread crumb crust. If you don't have a spice grinder, a clean coffee grinder will work just as well. (Grind the chile first and then make the bread crumbs in the grinder to clean it out.) Traditional mint jelly works fine as an accompaniment, but I like to surprise my guests with jalapeño jelly, which you can find in Latin markets and well-stocked supermarkets.

Tear the chile into small pieces and place them in a spice grinder. Grind the chile to a powder.

Melt the butter in a large heavy skillet over medium-high heat. Add the shallots and thyme and sauté for 3 minutes, or until the shallots are soft. Add the chile powder and stir. Add the bread crumbs and cook for 5 minutes, or until the crumbs are golden brown. Remove from the heat and season to taste with salt and pepper. Let the crumb topping cool.

Preheat the oven to 400°F.

Heat the olive oil in a large heavy skillet over high heat. Season the lamb racks all over with salt and pepper. Working in batches, add the lamb racks to the skillet, rounded side down. Sear for 6 minutes, or until brown. Transfer the racks to a large rimmed baking sheet, seared side up. Spread 1½ teaspoons of the mustard over each rack. Press the crumb topping into the mustard.

Roast for 20 minutes for medium-rare, or until desired doneness. Remove from the oven and let rest for 5 minutes before slicing into chops. Serve topped with jalapeño jelly, if desired.

SWEET POTATO GNOCCHI WITH SAGE BUTTER

1 pound sweet potatoes

2 tablespoons freshly grated Parmesan cheese, plus more for serving

⅛ teaspoon ground nutmeg

About 1¼ cups all-purpose flour, plus more for rolling

4 tablespoons (½ stick) unsalted butter

2 garlic cloves, minced

¼ cup chopped fresh sage

Salt and freshly ground black pepper

Making your own gnocchi is not as difficult or as time-consuming as you may think. Don't be afraid to try it! Sweet potatoes, a favorite Mexican ingredient, give the dough for these gnocchi a subtle sweetness and added nutrients (sweet potatoes are rich in fiber and vitamins A, B, and C). A simple butter-sage sauce is all you need to finish off this satisfying dish.

Preheat the oven to 400°F.

Wrap the sweet potatoes in foil, place them directly on the oven rack, and bake for 30 minutes, or until they are tender when pierced with a skewer. Let the sweet potatoes cool slightly. Then peel them and pass them through a potato ricer into a large bowl (if you don't have a potato ricer, you can mash them with a fork). Let the sweet potato puree cool completely.

Stir the Parmesan cheese and nutmeg into the sweet potato puree. Mix in enough flour to form a firm, slightly elastic dough. Turn the dough out onto a lightly floured surface. Divide the dough into 4 equal portions. Using your hands, gently roll 1 portion on the work surface to form a ½-inch-thick rope. Cut it crosswise into ½-inch pieces. Roll each piece over the tines of a dinner fork to form grooves. Arrange the gnocchi in a single layer on a floured baking sheet. Repeat with the remaining 3 portions of dough.

Bring a large pot of salted water to a boil. Working in 2 batches, cook the gnocchi in the boiling water for 4 minutes, or until they float and are tender. Use a slotted spoon to transfer them to a platter.

Meanwhile, melt the butter in a small saucepan. Add the garlic and cook over medium-low heat for 5 minutes, or until the garlic is fragrant. Add the sage and cook for 2 minutes, until crisp. Sprinkle with salt and pepper.

Spoon the butter sauce over the gnocchi, sprinkle with Parmesan cheese, and serve.

SIDES

THANKSGIVING . . . ON FRIDAY?

There's a reason I have no accent when I speak either English or Spanish: My mother wanted all of her children to take advantage of the fact that we lived on the U.S.–Mexico border, and during our formative years we moved back and forth between schools in San Diego and Tijuana.

I am happy to say that thanks to Mom, I can move seamlessly from English to Spanish. But I wasn't so lucky when it came to other subjects in school, like history. One year I would be learning about Benito Juárez and the next, George Washington. This could get a little confusing, particularly when it came to the celebration of national holidays.

My family is composed of Americans and Mexicans. Half of us live in San Diego and half of us live in Tijuana, but all of us celebrate *every* holiday, whether it is traditionally Mexican or American. I dressed up for Halloween on October 31, and I also had the day off on November 1 for Dia de Los Muertos.

My cousins from Guadalajara, much farther south in Mexico, were perplexed by our unique holiday traditions. We do not have Easter bunnies in Mexico, so looking for eggs that had been laid by bunnies seemed absurd to them. And what the hell was a tooth fairy? In Mexico, El Raton Perez (Perez the Mouse) rescued the lost teeth of children from under their pillows and left fifty pesos behind.

I thought all of this was fabulously hilarious but my dad, who is an old-school Mexican, had trouble embracing the ways of the North Americans. Not because he had anything against those traditions; he just already had his own and found no reason to adopt new ones. Take birthdays, for example. He doesn't really celebrate them. His mother, who was extremely religious, only celebrated her children's saint's days. All seventeen of them (yes, seventeen) were named after saints. My loving, kind, and generous father has no clue when my birthday is but I always get a phone call at 7 a.m. on the day of Santa Luz, after whom I am named Marcela Luz.

Over the years we've tried to observe all holidays, making small adjustments here and there to keep everybody happy, but suffice it to say, we sometimes run into trouble. Thanksgiving was the best example of our happy dilemma. Every year my dad points out what a confused bunch of Mexican-Americans we all are. We don't celebrate Thanksgiving in Mexico, so Mexican schoolchildren don't have the Friday after Thanksgiving off from school. Because we are a tequila, music, dancing, and firework-loving family (and because skipping class was not an option, per Dad), there is no way we could have Thanksgiving on a school night, so we just moved our annual Thanksgiving celebration to Friday.

My grandfather, Eugenio (also a chef), and my aunts assembled an extravagant meal consisting of dishes that had been passed down from both our American and Mexican ancestors. On the buffet table, the cranberry sauce sat next to the tamales. Brussels Sprouts in Morilla Cream (page 145) were a requirement for my dad. As soon as I was old enough to help in the kitchen (and had earned enough respect as a cook to be allowed to participate), dishes like Sage and Sweet Potato Mash (page 157) and Roasted Chipotle Acorn Squash (page 152) became favorites. It was an incredible night and it's one of the most treasured memories I have of my grandparents and the holidays at their house.

Many of the sides you'll see here are adaptations of the dishes served at that Thanksgiving table, or they are a fusion of two or more of those dishes. Like all the recipes in this book, they are meant to introduce you to a new way of looking at your favorite dishes and ingredients. I feel confident saying they make a wonderful addition to any dinner. Especially Thanksgiving dinner. Even if it's on Friday.

ROASTED CABBAGE WITH OREGANO AND OAXACA CHEESE

1 large cabbage, cut into 12 wedges

⅓ cup olive oil

2 tablespoons crumbled dried oregano

2 garlic cloves, minced

½ teaspoon salt

¼ teaspoon freshly ground black pepper

6 ounces Oaxaca cheese or mozzarella cheese, separated into long ½-inch-thick strings

Melted and slightly browned Oaxaca cheese mellows out bitter cabbage for this wonderful side dish. My son loves this with a little bit of lime juice sprinkled over it, and I like the edges, where the cheese is crisp and almost charred. When cutting the cabbage, cut on an angle so that there is a piece of the core on each wedge; it will hold the individual leaves together. For an impressive presentation, create a lattice with the strings of cheese.

Preheat the oven to 400°F.

Arrange the cabbage wedges, slightly overlapping, in a 9 x 13-inch glass baking dish. Mix the olive oil, oregano, garlic, salt, and pepper in a small bowl. Using a pastry brush, brush the olive oil mixture evenly over the cabbage wedges. Roast for 30 minutes, or until the cabbage begins to brown.

Remove the dish from the oven and reduce the oven temperature to 350°F.

Arrange the strings of cheese over the cabbage, forming a lattice if desired. Roast for 15 minutes, or until the cheese begins to brown. Serve hot.

BRUSSELS SPROUTS IN MORILLA CREAM

3 tablespoons unsalted butter

2 pounds brussels sprouts, halved

1 cup chicken broth

½ cup roasted salted sunflower seeds

3 scallions (white and pale green parts only), minced

1 morilla chile, stemmed, seeded, and very thinly sliced

½ cup heavy cream

Salt and freshly ground black pepper

It really *is* good to eat your brussels sprouts, and this morilla cream sauce, made with toasted sunflower seeds, will make a believer out of anyone. My father owns a plantation in San Quintín, Baja, where he grows and exports vegetables, including brussels sprouts. When I was young he would bring them home by the overflowing crateful—leaving me and my mother to come up with new, exciting ways to prepare them. This is my favorite recipe for serving the sprouts with a meal. For snacking, I love them coated with a little olive oil, sea salt, and black pepper and roasted until very crisp.

Melt 2 tablespoons of the butter in a large heavy saucepan over medium-high heat. Add the brussels sprouts and stir for 1 minute to coat them with the butter. Add the broth, cover, and simmer for 7 minutes, or until the brussels sprouts are tender. Uncover and continue to simmer for 4 minutes, or until all of the broth evaporates. Transfer the brussels sprouts to a medium bowl.

Melt the remaining 1 tablespoon butter in the same pan. Add the sunflower seeds, scallions, and chile and sauté for 2 minutes, or until the nuts are toasted and the chile is tender. Stir in the cream and bring to a boil. Reduce the heat, return the brussels sprouts to the pan, and toss to coat them with the cream. Season the brussels sprouts to taste with salt and pepper, and serve.

GRILLED VEGETABLES IN ESCABÈCHE

½ cup dry white wine

½ cup sherry vinegar

½ cup drained brine-cured green olives, pitted and halved

¼ cup fresh orange juice

2 tablespoons (packed) light brown sugar

2 tablespoons fresh lemon juice

2 tablespoons olive oil, plus additional for brushing the grill

1 tablespoon pickling spices

1 teaspoon salt

½ teaspoon dried hot red pepper flakes

3 small red bell peppers, stemmed, seeded, and cut into rings

3 small yellow bell peppers, stemmed, seeded, and cut into rings

1 red onion, cut into rings

2 carrots, thinly sliced on the diagonal

2 zucchini, thinly sliced on the diagonal

Pickled veggies show up on tables in many restaurants, bars, and homes across Mexico. These are great alongside meat, atop a quesadilla, or alone as a happy hour snack.

Prepare a grill or grill pan to medium-high heat.

Mix the wine, vinegar, olives, orange juice, brown sugar, lemon juice, olive oil, pickling spices, salt, and red pepper flakes in a large bowl to make the pickling juice.

Brush the grill lightly with olive oil. Grill all of the vegetables until tender but still firm to the bite.

Transfer the vegetables to the bowl with the pickling juice, and let them cool. Cover and refrigerate for at least 24 hours and up to 1 week before serving.

GRILLED CORN ON THE COB WITH JALAPEÑO BUTTER

2 jalapeño chiles

8 tablespoons (1 stick) unsalted butter, softened

1 garlic clove, minced

2 teaspoons minced fresh parsley

Salt and freshly ground black pepper

4 ears fresh corn, husks removed

1 cup crumbled queso fresco

Thankfully, in Tijuana we don't have to wait for summer to get the grill out. One of the benefits is that we can eat grilled corn on the cob any day of the year. Jalapeño butter is easy to make and adds the perfect finish to the slightly charred corn. If you have any left over, store it in the fridge for up to a week; it's great on a baked potato or green beans.

Prepare a grill or grill pan to high heat.

Grill the jalapeños, turning them occasionally, until charred on all sides, about 10 minutes. Transfer them to a cutting board and let cool for 5 minutes. (Keep the grill on.)

Using a small paring knife, peel the jalapeños. Scrape out and discard the seeds and veins. Coarsely chop the chiles and transfer them to a medium bowl. Add the butter, garlic, and parsley and mash together. Season the jalapeño butter to taste with salt and pepper. Place a square piece of plastic wrap on a work surface. Spoon the jalapeño butter onto the center and roll it up into a 1-inch-diameter log. Refrigerate it for at least 30 minutes, until set, or for up to 1 week.

Grill the corn, turning it occasionally, until it is browned in spots and the kernels are tender, about 15 minutes. Transfer the ears to a platter. Top each one with pat of the jalapeño butter, sprinkle with queso fresco, and serve.

CHORIZO-STUFFED CHAYOTE SQUASH

4 chayote squash (also called mirlitons; 2 pounds total)

3 ounces raw chorizo, casings removed

1 cup chopped onion

6 garlic cloves, minced

2 cups grated Manchego cheese (about 8 ounces)

Salt and freshly ground black pepper

¼ cup fresh bread crumbs

The state of Veracruz is the main growing region for chayote, a gourd that is eaten throughout Mexico and was once the principal food for Mayans and Aztecs. My family often serves it steamed, with a lime wedge. Here it is paired in perfect balance with spicy chorizo for an even tastier side dish.

Preheat the oven to 400°F.

Bring a large pot of salted water to a boil. Add the chayotes and boil for 50 minutes, or until tender when pierced with a fork. Drain the chayotes and let them cool slightly. Then cut the chayotes in half, removing and discarding the pit from each one. Carefully scoop out the flesh from each chayote and transfer it to a small bowl. Transfer the empty chayote skins to a baking sheet.

Cook the chorizo in a dry medium sauté pan over medium-high heat for 5 minutes, or until browned. Add the onion and garlic and cook for 8 minutes, or until the onion is translucent. Add the chayote flesh and half of the Manchego cheese, and stir to combine and melt the cheese. Season the filling to taste with salt and pepper, and remove from the heat.

Scoop the filling into the chayote skins, dividing it equally. Top with the remaining Manchego cheese, and sprinkle with the bread crumbs. Bake for 15 minutes, or until the cheese bubbles.

TORTA DE ELOTE
SOFT CORN BREAD

1 tablespoon unsalted butter, melted

12 tablespoons (1½ sticks) unsalted butter, softened

1 cup sugar

5 large egg yolks

8 cups fresh corn kernels (from 8 ears)

½ cup whole milk

6 tablespoons all-purpose flour

1 tablespoon baking powder

1 teaspoon salt

5 large egg whites

Every family in Mexico has its own version of this traditional soft corn bread. The classic recipe here is my favorite. Enjoy it as is, or experiment with sweet and savory versions by adding dried fruit or chopped jalapeños. Top sweeter versions with Creamed Rajas (page 188); savory versions are great with salsas. No matter how you make it, this Mexican delight is a perfect side for *carne asada.*

Preheat the oven to 350°F.

Grease a 9 x 13-inch glass baking dish with the melted butter.

Using an electric mixer, beat the 12 tablespoons butter and the sugar until pale and fluffy. Add the egg yolks, one at a time, blending well after each addition. Set aside, still in the mixer bowl.

Combine half of the corn kernels and half of the milk in a blender and puree to make a coarse creamy mixture. Transfer it to a large bowl. Repeat with the remaining corn and milk.

Mix the flour, baking powder, and salt in a small bowl.

Alternate adding the corn puree and the flour mixture to the butter mixture, mixing well after each addition. Transfer the mixture to a large bowl.

Using a clean electric mixer, whip the egg whites on high speed to form stiff peaks. Gently fold the egg whites into the corn mixture. Transfer the batter to the prepared baking dish, and bake for 1 hour and 20 minutes, or until the top is golden brown and a tester inserted into the center comes out clean. Let the corn bread cool slightly. Then cut it into squares and serve warm.

ROASTED CHIPOTLE ACORN SQUASH

2 acorn squash
(1½ to 1¾ pounds each)

2 tablespoons olive oil

2 garlic cloves, minced

1 teaspoon ground
chipotle chile

1 teaspoon salt

1 teaspoon freshly ground
black pepper

This dish is one of the standouts at the Valladolid Thanksgiving table. Roasting acorn squash—or any vegetable—caramelizes the flesh and brings out its natural sweetness. Your veggies will be exponentially more flavorful than they are when you boil or steam them.

Preheat the oven to 400°F.

Cut the acorn squash in half lengthwise. Then cut each half crosswise into ¾-inch-thick slices. Remove and discard the seeds from the squash pieces. Transfer the squash to a baking sheet.

Mix the olive oil, garlic, ground chipotle, salt, and pepper in a small bowl. Pour the mixture over the squash pieces and toss to coat.

Roast for 20 minutes, or until the squash is tender.

FRIJOLES DE LA OLLA

3 cups dried pinto beans

4 garlic cloves, mashed

¼ onion

2 bay leaves

Salt and freshly ground black pepper

I could easily survive on beans and tortillas for days—or even weeks. In fact, that is pretty much what my diet consisted of when I worked as a food editor. I was both nostalgic and barely able to make the rent at the end of the month, and let's face it, beans are cheap. *Frijoles de la olla* are just that: beans (*frijoles*) that come straight from the pot (*olla*) to your plate. No fussy seasonings, just perfectly cooked beans that are heaven in a warm tortilla with a drizzle of Mexican *crema* or sour cream. I always have a batch in the fridge to heat up for a hearty and very healthy dinner packed with cholesterol-lowering fiber and a good dose of protein, iron, potassium, and vitamin B_1.

Combine the beans, garlic, onion, and bay leaves in a medium pot. Add enough water to reach 2 fingers (about 1½ inches) over the beans. Bring to a boil over medium-high heat. Cover, and simmer until the beans are tender, about 2 hours, adding more water if the beans are absorbing too much liquid. (The beans should be soupy when done, with plenty of liquid remaining.) Season the beans to taste with salt and pepper. Serve with the cooking liquid as a soup. Or use a slotted spoon to drain to place in a tortilla for soft tacos. (The beans can be prepared 5 days ahead. Cool, cover, then refrigerate. Bring to a boil before serving.)

REFRIED BEANS

1 tablespoon unsalted butter

1 tablespoon olive oil

1 serrano chile, stemmed, halved, and seeded

1½ cups cooked Frijoles de la Olla (page 155), plus ½ cup cooking liquid

Salt and freshly ground black pepper

Refried beans are *frijoles de la olla* that have been fried in a little fat. Because they are traditionally cooked in lard, they aren't really known for their healthful qualities, but this version uses a fairly small amount of butter and olive oil instead. You still get a very rich and flavorful dish that is perfect for filling tacos or for serving alongside grilled steaks. Double or even quadruple this recipe as needed.

Melt the butter with the olive oil in a medium saucepan over medium-high heat. Add the serrano chile and cook for 1 minute, or until the chile is beginning to brown. Add the beans and the cooking liquid. Cook over medium heat, mashing the beans frequently, until they form a thick paste, about 10 minutes. Season to taste with salt and pepper.

SAGE AND SWEET POTATO MASH

2 pounds sweet potatoes

1 cup whole milk, warmed to lukewarm

8 tablespoons (1 stick) unsalted butter, softened

1 teaspoon olive oil

½ cup chopped fresh sage

4 garlic cloves, minced

Salt and freshly ground black pepper

Sweet potatoes cooked in *piloncillo* (unrefined solid cane sugar, usually found in the shape of small truncated cones) are sold as candy at Mexican *mercados*. They are way too sweet for me, but there's no denying the spud's versatility. Here I highlight their savory flavor by mashing sweet potatoes with a little butter and sage in a great fall dish that works well with roasted turkey. Feel free to use skim milk instead of whole milk, if you must, but keep that stick of butter!

Bring a large pot of salted water to a boil. Add the sweet potatoes and boil for 25 minutes, or until tender when pierced with a fork. Drain and let cool slightly.

Peel the potatoes and transfer the flesh to a large bowl. Mash in the milk and 7 tablespoons of the butter. Set aside.

Melt the remaining 1 tablespoon butter with the oil in a small heavy saucepan over medium-high heat. Add the sage and garlic and cook for 4 minutes, or until fragrant. Stir this into the potato mixture. Season the mash to taste with salt and pepper. (The mash can be prepared 1 day ahead and refrigerated. Stir in a saucepan over medium-low heat, adding more milk if necessary, until heated through.)

POBLANO RICE GRATIN

2 tablespoons
vegetable oil

¼ cup minced white onion

1 cup long-grain
white rice

Kernels from 2 ears
fresh corn

2 poblano chiles, charred
(see page 35), stemmed,
seeded, and chopped

¼ cup Mexican *crema*
(see page 70) or sour
cream

½ cup grated Monterey
Jack cheese

This spicy, cheesy rice dish was served on a regular basis at my parents' house. It's also perfectly delicious if you prefer to omit the *crema* and cheese and just serve the poblano rice on its own, saving you a few calories.

Heat the oil in a medium-size heavy skillet over medium-high heat. Add the onion and sauté for 5 minutes, or until translucent. Add the rice and cook for 10 minutes, or until the rice is opaque. Add 2 cups water and the corn kernels, and bring to a boil. Reduce the heat to medium-low, cover, and simmer for 15 minutes, or until the rice is tender.

Meanwhile, preheat the broiler on high.

When the rice is cooked, fluff it with a fork and stir in the chopped poblanos. Transfer the rice to a 7 x 10-inch glass baking dish. Drizzle with the *crema,* and sprinkle the cheese all over the rice. Broil for 8 to 10 minutes, or until the top is browned in spots and the cheese has melted.

ANCHO AND PINE NUT RICE

3½ cups chicken broth

2 ancho chiles, stemmed and seeded

¼ cup whole milk

½ teaspoon salt

½ teaspoon freshly ground black pepper

1 tablespoon unsalted butter

1 tablespoon olive oil

1 cup chopped onion

2 garlic cloves, minced

½ cup pine nuts

1½ cups medium-grain rice

This is one of my favorite ways to eat rice: spicy and with nuts! The spice from the chiles is perfectly balanced by earthy pine nuts. To cut down on the heat, you can always use one ancho chile instead of two, but I encourage you to try it with two the first time around. You might be surprised at how well the flavors work together. Because they are picked by hand, pine nuts can be expensive. Feel free to substitute chopped or slivered almonds instead.

Bring the chicken broth to a boil in a medium-size heavy saucepan over high heat. Add the ancho chiles and remove from the heat. Let stand for 15 minutes, or until the chiles soften.

Transfer the chiles and broth to a blender and puree until smooth. Strain into a 4-cup measuring cup to measure 2¾ cups (reserve the remaining puree for another use). Add the milk, salt, and pepper and set aside.

Melt the butter with the olive oil in a medium saucepan over medium-high heat. Add the onion and garlic and sauté for 3 minutes, or until the onion is translucent. Add the pine nuts and stir for 2 minutes, or until they are golden. Add the rice and stir for 2 minutes, or until it is coated with oil.

Add the ancho puree and bring to a boil. Cover, reduce the heat to low, and simmer for 20 minutes, or until all the liquid has been absorbed. Remove the pan from the heat and let the rice stand for 5 minutes. Then fluff the rice with a fork and serve.

ÁRBOL CHILE—INFUSED COUSCOUS WITH DATES AND ORANGES

1½ cups vegetable broth

2 dried árbol chiles

One 3-inch-long cinammon stick

1 cup plain couscous

3 oranges

¼ cup pine nuts, toasted

¼ cup chopped pitted dates

¼ cup minced red onion

3 tablespoons chopped fresh cilantro

2 tablespoons olive oil

Salt and freshly ground black pepper

Couscous, made from semolina, is a staple in North African cuisine. Here it is infused with spicy chiles and cinnamon in this easy-to-whip-up salad that would pair nicely with grilled lamb or poultry.

Combine the broth, chiles, and cinnamon stick in a medium-size heavy saucepan over medium-high heat, and bring to a boil. Remove the pan from the heat and let stand for 5 minutes. Then remove and discard the chiles and cinnamon stick.

Put the couscous in a large bowl and pour the hot infused broth over it. Cover, and let stand for 4 minutes.

Meanwhile, cut the peel and white pith from each orange. Working over a medium bowl, cut between the membranes to release the orange segments. Reserve 1 tablespoon of the orange juice.

Fluff the couscous with a fork. Mix in the orange segments, pine nuts, dates, onion, cilantro, olive oil, and the reserved orange juice. Season the couscous salad to taste with salt and pepper. Serve warm, at room temperature, or chilled.

SALSAS

LAS SALSAS

Poblano, serrano, morilla, chilaca, California, mulato, ancho, cascabel, chipotle, habanero, jalapeño, de árbol, mirasol, pasilla, chiltepín, piquín . . . Mexican chiles provide inspiration for a near-endless list of salsas.

I once read that if tortillas are the heart of Mexico, then salsas are the blood, and I completely agree. For me, they are what best differentiates Mexican food from any other cuisine in the world. Some salsas are grilled, some are fried, some are raw, some are sweet. They all add flavor and dimension to any meal. It's like eating ketchup with French fries. To the classic Mexican dishes—quesadillas, tacos de carne asada, huevos rancheros—salsa is the final touch that makes the food that much better.

And what makes a good salsa? A perfect combination of chiles. Use dried when looking for smoky and nutty undertones. Go for fresh for brighter flavors. If you aren't sure which to choose, a good rule for beginners is that the smaller the chile, the spicier the kick. The best advice I could ever give to anyone concerning chiles is to be brave enough to try them. Start by just putting the tip of your tongue to the chile: you'll get a very good sense of the spice and the flavor. Remove the veins if you like your salsas on the mild side; that's where most of the heat is hiding.

The first thing that comes to mind when people think of salsa is the chunky dip for tortilla chips (which I absolutely love when both the chips and the salsa are homemade), but there is so much more to explore. In this chapter you will find some of my favorites, including Salsa Borracha (page 170), which I developed for my show on Discovery en Español: tequila, ancho chiles, and fresh orange juice are cooked down to a smoky sweet sauce with incredible depth that will absolutely surprise and delight your palate. Topped with crumbled añejo cheese and stuffed in a warm tortilla right off the *comal*—it just doesn't get any better.

If you think it's easier to purchase your salsa in a jar, let me prove you wrong. For the recipes in this book, I have purposely omitted the use of a *molcajete* (mortar and pestle), the traditional tool for making salsa, and call for a blender or processor in its

place. The truth is, while the processor blade cuts through the ingredients, a molcajete presses and grinds to release natural juices and flavorings, yielding superior flavor and texture. But at the risk of upsetting my ancestors, my priority is for you to actually *make* these salsas. If you do happen to have a molcajete, go ahead and use it. If not, don't let that stop you.

In addition to recipes for traditional salsas, I have included a few straight from my own kitchen, and my own cravings. For example, anyone who knows me knows I could eat an entire jar of mayonnaise. I haven't actually done this yet, but you can bet if I attempt it, it will be the homemade chipotle mayonnaise on page 187. I love it for chicken salad or for spreading on tostadas, and I am always mixing stuff into it, like roasted jalapeños and capers.

The idea with salsas is to have fun. After you make one successful salsa, you'll want to try another, and another. Before long, salsa will be as natural (and essential) to your meals as ketchup is to those French fries.

ROASTED TOMATILLO– CILANTRO SALSA

1½ pounds tomatillos, husked, rinsed, and halved

2 small onions, quartered

1 serrano chile, halved, stemmed, and seeded

2 tablespoons olive oil

Salt and freshly ground black pepper

1 head garlic, wrapped tightly in aluminum foil

½ cup chicken broth

½ avocado, halved, pitted, peeled, and diced

3 tablespoons chopped fresh cilantro

A fresh *salsa verde,* or green sauce, made with tomatillos is a perfect condiment for almost any meal (I like it on grilled chicken tacos), and just as good as a dip for tortilla chips.

Preheat the oven to 350°F.

Put the tomatillos, onions, and serrano chile on a baking sheet, all cut side up. Drizzle with the olive oil and sprinkle generously with salt and pepper. Put the foil-wrapped garlic on the same baking sheet. Roast for 45 minutes, or until the garlic and vegetables are soft and the edges of the vegetables are beginning to brown. Let cool slightly.

Transfer the tomatillos, onions, and serrano chile to a blender. Unwrap the garlic and squeeze the garlic cloves from their papery skins into the blender. Add the broth, and puree to a chunky texture. (The salsa can be made 1 day ahead up to this point. Cool, cover, and refrigerate.)

Before serving, fold the avocado and cilantro into the salsa, and season to taste with salt and pepper.

TOMATILLOS

A tomatillo is a small green fruit encased in
a tissue-paper-like husk (which is why it is
sometimes called the husk-tomato). Indigenous
to Mexico, tomatillos have been used in cooking
since pre-Columbian times. They continue to be a
staple in Mexican cuisine, and they are the main
ingredient in salsa verde. As the Latino population
in the United States increases, tomatillos
are becoming more readily available in large
supermarkets.

Tomatillos should be used when they are still
green, before they are ripe and the husk has
turned brown. Before using them, remove the husk
and then rinse and dry the fruit thoroughly (they
do not need to be seeded).

Mini tomatillos, harder to find, are about the size
of a cherry tomato and can be used in place of
regular tomatillos, with slightly sweeter results.

SALSA BORRACHA

8 ancho chiles

½ cup fresh orange juice

½ cup golden tequila

1 garlic clove, minced

4 tablespoons olive oil

Salt and freshly ground black pepper

¼ cup crumbled añejo or feta cheese

"Drunken" salsas have been around forever. They were originally prepared with *pulque*, an alcoholic beverage made from the fermented juice of the once-sacred maguey (agave) plant. Pulque, which is not easy to find outside of Mexico, is not distilled and has a much stronger flavor than tequila, which I use in its place in this recipe. The alcohol is mostly burned off in the cooking process, leaving only its musky flavor. The sweetness from the freshly squeezed orange juice gives this salsa a wonderful balance.

Cook the chiles in a dry sauté pan over high heat, turning them constantly, for 2 minutes, or until slightly toasted. Halve and seed the chiles. Tear them into small pieces and transfer the pieces to a blender.

Add the orange juice, tequila, garlic, and 2 tablespoons of the olive oil to the blender. Puree until the salsa is nearly smooth.

Heat the remaining 2 tablespoons olive oil in a sauté pan over high heat. Add the salsa and cook for 5 minutes, or until slightly thickened. Season the salsa with salt and pepper. Let it cool completely. (The salsa can be made 1 day ahead. Cover the sauce and keep it in the fridge.)

Serve the salsa topped with the crumbled añejo cheese.

SMOKED SALMON— CHILE MULATO SAUCE

2 tablespoons olive oil

2 mulato chiles, stemmed, seeded, and torn into pieces

2 garlic cloves

1 cup heavy cream

8 ounces smoked salmon, thinly sliced

2 red bell peppers, charred (see page 35), stemmed, peeled, seeded, and chopped

Salt and freshly ground black pepper

¼ cup thinly sliced fresh basil

The smoked salmon gives this sauce great texture and is also a wonderful flavor complement to the smokiness of the chile mulato. Try the sauce on pasta or with a char-grilled chicken breast.

Heat the olive oil in a medium-size heavy saucepan over medium heat. Add the chiles and garlic cloves and swirl in the oil for 2 minutes, or until the garlic is golden brown and the chiles are fragrant. Add the cream, smoked salmon, and chopped bell peppers and bring to a boil. Reduce the heat to medium-low and simmer for 4 minutes, or until the sauce thickens.

Transfer the sauce to a blender and puree until smooth. Season with salt and pepper. Stir in the fresh basil. Serve hot.

GRILLED PINEAPPLE SALSA

½ ripe but firm pineapple, peeled, cored, and cut into ½-inch-thick slices

¼ cup chopped fresh cilantro

½ serrano chile, stemmed, seeded, and diced

1 tablespoon fresh lime juice

Pinch of sugar, or to taste

Salt and freshly ground black pepper

My aunt Martha swears that this smoky, sweet, tropical salsa takes her back to Yucatán no matter where she is when she makes it. It works especially well with Cilantro Tandoori Chicken (page 110), but it will enhance any grilled fish or meat. If the grill's fired up, throw the pineapple right on it; a grill pan will do just fine if you're cooking indoors.

Prepare a grill or grill pan to medium-high heat.

Grill the pineapple slices for 2 minutes per side, or until tender and grill-marked. Transfer the slices to a cutting board and chop them. Put the chopped pineapple in a medium bowl and stir in the cilantro, serrano chile, and lime juice. Season the salsa to taste with sugar, salt, and pepper. Serve warm.

SESAME SEED AND ÁRBOL CHILE SALSA

1½ tablespoons
vegetable oil

¼ cup minced onion

2 large garlic cloves

¼ cup sesame seeds,
toasted (see Tips,
page 23)

½ cup dried árbol chiles

4 large tomatillos, husked
and rinsed

Salt and freshly ground
black pepper

Nuts and seeds have been making their way into Mexican sauces and salsas for centuries. The nutty sesame seeds in this salsa, which is served at a very popular small restaurant in Tijuana called Mi Rincón Cenaduria (My Restaurant Nook), give it body and depth. Use this on steak tacos or even with grilled chicken. Peanuts can be substituted for the sesame seeds.

Heat the vegetable oil in a large heavy sauté pan over medium-high heat. Add the onion and garlic cloves and sauté for 5 minutes, or until the garlic is golden brown. Add the sesame seeds and árbol chiles and cook for 5 minutes, or until the chiles are darkened in spots.

Meanwhile, heat a medium-size heavy sauté pan over high heat. Add the tomatillos and cook, turning them frequently, for 10 minutes, or until they are pale green and blackened in spots. Add the tomatillos to the chile mixture in the pan, pressing on them with a spatula to break them apart and release their juices. Cook for 5 minutes to blend the flavors. Remove from the heat and let cool slightly.

Transfer the contents of the pan to a blender, and add 1½ cups water. Blend until the salsa is smooth. Season to taste with salt and pepper. Cool to room temperature, and then serve.

THREE CHILE SALSA

2 tablespoons
vegetable oil

3 guajillo chiles,
stemmed, seeded, and
torn into pieces

4 cascabel chiles,
stemmed, seeded, and
torn into pieces

3 dried árbol chiles,
stemmed, seeded, and
torn into pieces

3 large garlic cloves

2 tablespoons chopped
fresh cilantro

Salt and freshly ground
black pepper

What's better than one chile? Three! Mexican food owes much of its flair to the chile, which has been around since about 7500 B.C. Chiles add heat and depth to almost everything I make at home. (As an added bonus, some scientists believe the chile has miraculous disease-fighting powers, with the ability to promote weight loss and to prevent everything from heart disease to cancer.) Here you have the cascabel chile, which adds a slightly nutty flavor, the árbol chile, which brings heat, and my favorite, the sweet and smoky guajillo, to create a salsa that is in perfect harmony.

Heat the oil in a large heavy pan over medium-high heat. Add all three kinds of chiles and sauté for 3 minutes, or until fragrant. Transfer the chiles to a medium bowl and add water to cover. Let stand for 30 minutes, or until the chiles are soft.

Drain the chiles (discard the soaking liquid) and transfer them to a blender. Add the garlic, cilantro, and ½ cup water, and blend until the salsa is smooth. Season to taste with salt and pepper. Cool to room temperature, and serve.

CHILES TOREADOS
FRIED CHILES WITH LIME-SOY SAUCE

Vegetable oil, for frying

2 pounds güero chiles

½ cup fresh lime juice

½ cup soy sauce

2 tablespoons Asian oyster sauce

Every family has a recipe that is a well-kept secret. This one, created by my aunt Marcela, is ours. It took some major coaxing to convince her to let me in on the details. Chile-lovers, this is for you! Yellow chiles are left whole and are meant to be eaten in between bites of tacos or any grilled dish. If you want to get adventurous, try dipping sushi in the spicy lime-soy sauce.

Pour enough vegetable oil into a medium-size heavy saucepan to reach halfway up the sides of the pan. Heat the oil to 350°F. Working in batches, fry the chiles in the hot oil until golden, about 4 minutes. Transfer them to paper towels to drain.

Mix the lime juice, soy sauce, and oyster sauce in a medium bowl. Add the warm chiles and toss to combine. Chill for 3 hours or until very cold. (The chiles will keep in the refrigerator for up to 1 week.)

CILANTRO PESTO

2 cups (packed) cilantro leaves

¾ cup (packed) añejo or feta cheese

½ cup roasted salted sunflower seeds

2 tablespoons fresh lime juice

½ jalapeño chile, stemmed and seeded

¾ cup olive oil

Salt and freshly ground black pepper

Traditional basil pesto gets a run for its money with this bright, flavorful Mexican version of the Italian original. Cilantro pesto is best on cold pasta salads and is great as a topping on grilled chicken or fish.

Combine the cilantro, cheese, sunflower seeds, lime juice, and jalapeño in a food processor and pulse to combine. With the machine running, gradually add the olive oil. Season the pesto to taste with salt and pepper. Cover and refrigerate for up to 2 hours. Bring to room temperature and stir before using.

MANGO, SERRANO, AND AVOCADO SALSA

1 mango, peeled, pitted, and diced

2 avocados, halved, pitted, peeled, and diced

1 serrano chile, charred (see page 35), stemmed, seeded, and diced

1 tablespoon chopped fresh cilantro

2 teaspoons fresh lime juice

Salt and freshly ground black pepper

Mangoes sprinkled with a mixture of chile and salt and served on a stick are popular street-corner fare in Mexico. I love the combination of flavors so much that I used it to create this salsa, with the addition of avocado for extra richness. Mangoes come in several varieties, and any type will work as long as the fruit is ripe but firm enough that it won't fall apart in the salsa.

Gently mix the mango, avocados, serrano chile, cilantro, and lime juice in a bowl. Season the salsa to taste with salt and pepper. Serve immediately.

FRESH TOMATILLO-AVOCADO SALSA

8 ounces tomatillos, husked, rinsed, and roughly chopped

1 avocado, halved, pitted, and peeled

½ cup (packed) fresh cilantro leaves

1 serrano chile

1 tablespoon fresh lemon juice

Salt and freshly ground black pepper

Tomatillo salsas vary greatly from region to region in Mexico. Some are boiled, some are fried, some are roasted, but all of them have the same distinct acidic taste that makes the tomatillo one of Mexico's trademark ingredients. A batch of this salsa is made daily at my house; it's always in my fridge. It's my topping of choice for quesadillas.

Combine the tomatillos, avocado, cilantro, serrano chile, and lemon juice in a blender and puree until smooth. Season the salsa to taste with salt and pepper. Refrigerate for up to 2 hours or until ready to use.

GOLDEN PICO DE GALLO

1½ pounds yellow tomatoes, seeded and chopped

¾ cup chopped onion

½ cup chopped fresh cilantro

3 tablespoons fresh lime juice

2 serrano chiles, stemmed, seeded, and minced

Salt and freshly ground black pepper

In Mexico *pico de gallo* is used to describe a wide variety of regional salsas, which are always made with cubed fresh fruit and/or vegetables. Pico de gallo is also known as *salsa picada,* which means minced or chopped sauce. The most common version is made with red tomatoes, onion, and green chiles and is sometimes called *salsa mexicana* or *salsa bandera,* because the colors in the salsa represent those of the Mexican flag. I like to make mine with yellow tomatoes when I am in the mood for a sweeter salsa. Feel free to use red tomatoes if you want to keep it traditional.

Mix the tomatoes, onion, cilantro, lime juice, and serrano chiles in a medium bowl. Season with salt and pepper. Cover and chill for at least 30 minutes, until the flavors blend. (The salsa can be made 4 hours ahead.)

PICKLED ONIONS

1 red onion, thinly sliced

¾ cup distilled white vinegar

6 tablespoons sugar

½ teaspoon crumbled dried oregano

½ teaspoon salt

In Mexico, pickled onions are to taco stands what pickle relish is to a hot dog cart in the U.S.—a condiment that taco-lovers can't do without. Make it at home and save yourself the trip across the border.

Combine the onion, vinegar, sugar, oregano, salt, and ¾ cup water in a large self-seal plastic bag. Shake the bag to combine the ingredients. Let the onion marinate for at least 24 hours and up to 4 days in the refrigerator.

HOMEMADE CHIPOTLE MAYO

2 large egg yolks

1 tablespoon fresh lemon juice

1 canned chipotle chile in adobo, plus 3 teaspoons of the adobo sauce

1 teaspoon Dijon mustard

1¼ cups corn oil

1 teaspoon salt

½ teaspoon freshly ground black pepper

I am obsessed with mayo, especially homemade mayo. All it takes is a little patience, and the end result is much brighter and smoother than any store-bought variety. It's traditionally made by hand, by vigorously beating with a whisk, but I make it in a food processor, which is much easier. I always have a batch of this chipotle mayo in the fridge; you can easily omit the chipotles for a mayo base to which you could add any sort of flavorings. Raw eggs are used in this recipe, so it's best to not serve this to pregnant women, children, or anyone with a compromised immune system. If you use pasteurized egg yolks, however, you can serve it to whomever you like.

Combine the egg yolks, lemon juice, chipotle chile, adobo sauce, and Dijon mustard in a food processor, and pulse two or three times to combine. With the machine running, add the oil in a very slow, steady stream until all of the oil has been incorporated (this should take about 5 minutes). Add the salt and pepper and pulse to combine. Store, covered, in the refrigerator for up to 1 week.

CREAMED RAJAS

3 tablespoons
vegetable oil

1 medium white onion,
thinly sliced

2 cups fresh corn kernels
(from 2 ears)

6 poblano chiles, charred
(see page 35), peeled,
stemmed, seeded, and
cut into strips

¼ cup heavy cream

¼ cup Mexican *crema*
(page 70) or crème
fraîche

½ cup shredded Oaxaca
cheese or mozzarella
cheese

Salt and freshly ground
black pepper

A great filling for tacos or topping for any grilled meat, these creamy poblano strips (*rajas*) showed up on the table a few times a week while I was growing up. You can cream virtually any chile, but mild poblanos add the perfect amount of spice to any dish. My favorite pairing is with sweet Torta de Elote (page 153).

Heat the oil in a large heavy skillet over medium heat. Add the onion and sauté for 5 minutes, or until translucent. Add the corn kernels and cook for an additional 3 minutes.

Add the chile strips to the corn mixture and cook for 5 minutes, or until the corn is tender. Add the heavy cream and *crema* and cook for 8 minutes, or until bubbling. Add the cheese and stir until melted and smooth. Season the *rajas* to taste with salt and pepper. Serve hot. (The *rajas* can be made 1 day ahead. Cool, cover, and refrigerate. Stir over medium heat until hot before serving.)

DESSERTS

LA DULCE AFICIONADA

On more than one occasion as a young girl, I walked into the kitchen to find my older sister, Carina, pouring *cajeta,* a caramel spread made with goat's milk, straight into her mouth. "How can you do that?" I would protest with absolute horror. "It's all sugar!" I wasn't concerned about her health—I just couldn't fathom eating a container of sticky caramel without stopping for air.

I soon understood that Carina is a very strange creature who can go for days on sugar alone. She's known to stash chocolate underneath her bed, and when she feels it's gotten out of hand, she'll ask someone to hide it from her for a couple of days. Hide, not throw away, mind you. I used to have this peculiar job. Now I think it's been relegated to her poor husband, Raymundo, who has lectured my sister many, many times on the questionable example she's setting for their three young girls, Isabella, Daniella, and Gabriella.

Raymundo is the rare type of guy who likes to whisk his wife off to San Francisco or Las Vegas, just to eat at the fanciest restaurants and order the chef's special menu paired with the restaurant's finest wines. I always imagine Carina on one of those culinary adventures, pretending to love her pork chop while secretly waiting for the dessert to arrive. She calls me every morning after these dinners and tries, to the best of her ability, to recount each course. She usually forgets half of them but is always able to give me incredible details on the taste, texture, presentation, and aroma of the dessert and each of its components!

It wasn't until I spent the summer in Paris and studied classic French pastry at the Ritz-Escoffier cooking school that I began to understand my sister's obsession. I wasn't much interested in sweets when I was growing up, preferring the more salty-sour candy varieties from local candy stores. It was in Paris that I learned to appreciate an ethereal flaky dough, the gloss of expertly tempered chocolate, or a perfectly cooked caramel. My love and understanding of sugar was established then and there.

Although not obsessed like my unusually petite redheaded sugar *aficionada* of a sister, I now find myself sneaking into the kitchen every once in a while with a craving for something sweet. Although I will never resort to squirting the *cajeta* straight into my mouth, I will, however, fill a very large spoon with the sweet caramel and bring it upstairs to nibble on while reading a book or typing up a recipe.

As for the desserts in this book, know one thing: They all have Carina's stamp of approval. I had to remake the Amaranth Macaroons (page 200) a few times before getting the perfect almond-to-sugar ratio *and* her blessing. I adore my nieces, but Carina being pregnant translated to my making a whole bunch of Mexican Chocolate Soufflé (page 219) and Pomegranate Pine Nut Brittle (page 222). Have you ever tried to tell a pregnant woman with cravings that you're too busy to be making desserts on demand? I wouldn't recommend it.

Carina's lifelong obsession with anything and everything sweet has made her a connoisseur of confections, and she has become much more discriminating with time. Thumbs-up from her guarantees a home run. And guess what? She has tasted, and approved, every single one of these recipes. If there is an ingredient that's not to be found in your local grocery store, go out of your way to find it. Believe me, it's worth it. Especially the *cajeta* . . .

BUÑUELOS

BUÑUELOS

½ cup sugar

1 teaspoon ground cinnamon

Vegetable oil, for frying

Six 8-inch flour tortillas, whole or cut into shapes

The smell of fried tortillas and cinnamon engulfed our home during the Christmas season as my mom made dozens of these crunchy treats and wrapped them in cellophane to give to friends and family. I've now taken over the tradition, and my son loves to help me cut the tortillas into holiday shapes with cookie cutters or scissors before I fry them. Using authentic Mexican tortillas (lard and all) makes all the difference.

Mix the sugar and cinnamon together on a plate.

Pour enough oil into a medium-size heavy saucepan to reach halfway up the sides of the pan. Heat the oil to 350°F.

Working in batches, fry the tortillas in the hot oil for 2 minutes on each side, until golden brown. Transfer them to paper towels to drain. While the tortillas are still warm, toss them with the cinnamon sugar, turning to coat. Serve warm, preferably, or at room temperature.

POLVORONES
GROUND WALNUT COOKIES

1 cup (2 sticks) unsalted butter, at room temperature

½ cup granulated sugar

2 cups all-purpose flour

½ cup ground walnuts

1 cup chopped walnuts

½ cup powdered sugar, plus more for serving (optional)

Polvo means "powder" in Spanish, which is exactly what these crumbly, buttery cookies turn into in your mouth. My mom made polvorones for us every Christmas. These melt-in-your-mouth Mexican wedding cookies are very easy to prepare and are the perfect accompaniment to a cup of after-dinner coffee—or for dipping in hot chocolate, as I did when I was a child.

Using an electric mixer, beat the butter in a large bowl until light and fluffy. Add the granulated sugar and beat until well blended. Beat in the flour, then the ground and chopped walnuts. Divide the dough in half, forming each half into a ball. Wrap them separately in plastic wrap, and refrigerate until cold, about 30 minutes.

Preheat the oven to 325°F. Put the ½ cup powdered sugar in a shallow bowl and set it aside.

Working with half of the chilled dough at a time and keeping the rest in the fridge, roll 2-teaspoon-size chunks of the dough between your palms to form balls. Arrange the balls on a large baking sheet, spacing them ½ inch apart.

Bake the cookies until they are golden brown on the bottom and just pale golden on top, about 18 minutes. Let the cookies cool on the baking sheet for 5 minutes. Then toss the warm cookies in the powdered sugar. Transfer the sugar-coated cookies to a rack to cool completely. (The cookies can be prepared 2 days ahead. Store them in an airtight container at room temperature.)

Sift additional powdered sugar over the cookies, if desired, before serving.

MANGO POCKETS WITH CINNAMON CREAM

20 wonton wrappers

1 large ripe but firm mango, peeled, pitted, and diced

1 large egg, lightly beaten

Vegetable oil, for frying

⅔ cup plus 2 tablespoons sugar

3 teaspoons ground cinnamon

½ cup heavy cream

This delectable fritter was a happy accident. My friend (and loyal assistant) Valeria suggested I prepare a mango ravioli for this book. She envisioned a dough made with mango puree, but I misunderstood and made a mango filling. This miscommunication, coupled with my obsession with the very versatile wonton wrapper, brought a new dessert to life!

Place a wonton wrapper on a work surface, and spoon 3 or 4 small pieces of mango onto the center. Brush the edges of the wonton with a little of the beaten egg. Fold in half on the diagonal. Then fold all the corners in so they touch, to resemble a small pouch, pressing on the edges to seal. Repeat with the remaining wonton wrappers and mango.

Pour enough oil into a medium saucepan to reach halfway up the sides of the pan. Heat the oil to 350°F.

Stir the ⅔ cup sugar and 2 teaspoons of the cinnamon together on a baking sheet.

Working in batches, fry the mango pockets in the hot oil for 4 minutes, or until crisp and golden brown. Transfer them to paper towels to drain. Then, while the mango pockets are still warm, transfer them to the baking sheet and toss them in the cinnamon sugar to coat.

Combine the cream, remaining 2 tablespoons sugar, and remaining 1 teaspoon cinnamon in a medium bowl and whisk to form soft peaks.

Serve the mango pockets with the cinnamon cream for dipping.

AMARANTH MACAROONS

1½ cups ground blanched almonds

2½ cups powdered sugar

3 large egg whites

2 tablespoons granulated sugar

¼ teaspoon cream of tartar

½ cup amaranth seeds (see page 202)

My very close friend and colleague Elsa Flores, a Baja pastry chef, shared this recipe with me. It's a wonderful fusion of one very Mexican ingredient, amaranth, with one very French dessert, macaroons. Be sure to let the raw macaroons rest after they are piped. This will dry out the tops and will result in a shinier and perfectly puffed macaroon.

Preheat the oven to 200°F. Line a baking sheet with parchment paper.

Combine the ground almonds and powdered sugar in a food processor, and process until the mixture is very fine.

Using an electric mixer, whip the egg whites in a large bowl until foamy. With the machine running, gradually beat in the granulated sugar. Add the cream of tartar and whip to form stiff peaks. Sift the ground almond mixture over the beaten egg whites, and use a rubber spatula to carefully fold it in.

Using a pastry bag fitted with a ½-inch-diameter tip, pipe 1-inch rounds (they will expand slightly) 1½ inches apart on the prepared baking sheet. Sprinkle the tops of the macaroons with the amaranth seeds. Let the uncooked macaroons stand at room temperature for 15 minutes.

Bake the macaroons for 10 minutes. Then rotate the baking sheet and bake for 12 minutes longer, or until the macaroons are puffed and the tops appear dry (macaroons should be crisp on the outside and chewy on the inside). Let the macaroons cool on the baking sheet for 15 minutes before removing them from the parchment. Store in an airtight container at room temperature for up to 2 days.

AMARANTH

Aztecs and Incas believed amaranth had magical and medicinal properties and used it in rituals involving human blood. The Spanish conquistadors, afraid of this pagan practice, burned down all the amaranth crops.

Found to be high in fiber, calcium, iron, and potassium, amaranth has recently been described as the power "grain" (it is technically a grass) for underweight children in underdeveloped countries, especially since it's relatively easy to grow. In Mexico and in health food stores in the U.S., you can find the raw seeds on their own or sweetened with honey; either can be used in the recipe on page 200.

MOM'S STRAWBERRY TARTLETS

1½ cups hulled quartered strawberries

½ cup plus 3 tablespoons granulated sugar

Nonstick cooking spray

5 ounces Maria crackers (about 32 crackers; see page 205) or graham crackers (about 10 whole crackers)

¼ cup (packed) minced piloncillo (about 2 ounces) or dark brown sugar

8 tablespoons (1 stick) cold unsalted butter, cubed

Two 8-ounce packages cream cheese, at room temperature

½ cup sour cream

My mom made a variation of this dessert from the time I was a little girl. I'm not exactly sure where she got the recipe, but I know it came from one of my aunts in Guadalajara. You just need to know that my uncle Ernesto would drive from his house in San Diego across the border into Tijuana to go to my mom's house when she announced she was making strawberry pie. It's not traditional or very Mexican, especially in its original form. She used to use a store-bought graham-cracker pie crust (which you are free to use), but I have concocted a much tastier crust using the traditional Maria cracker and piloncillo (unrefined solid cane sugar, usually found in the shape of small truncated cones). What I absolutely left alone is the filling—a fluffy, creamy, perfectly sweet filling that I could eat an entire bowl of if given a spoon. The amounts given will also work with a 9-inch round tart pan with removable bottom if you don't want to make individual tartlets.

Mix the strawberries and the 3 tablespoons granulated sugar in a small bowl to combine. Let the strawberries macerate at room temperature for 1 hour.

Preheat the oven to 350°F. Place six 3½ x ¾-inch tartlet pans with removable bottoms on a baking sheet. Spray the tartlet pans with nonstick cooking spray.

RECIPE CONTINUES

Combine the crackers and piloncillo in a food processor, and process to form coarse crumbs. Add the butter and process until the crumbs come together. Press the crumbs into the prepared tartlet pans. Bake for 10 minutes, or until the tartlet shells are golden brown. Let them cool completely.

Using an electric mixer, whip the cream cheese and sour cream in a bowl until fluffy. Add the remaining ½ cup granulated sugar and whip until well combined. Drain the strawberries from the macerating liquid, reserving 2 tablespoons of the liquid. Fold the strawberries and the reserved liquid into the cream cheese mixture. Spoon the strawberry filling into the tartlet shells, dividing it equally. (The tarts can be prepared 1 day ahead. Cover and refrigerate.)

GALLETAS MARIAS

Maria crackers are round sweet cookies with a vanilla flavor. They are the Mexican version of the English Marie biscuit. One of the most popular methods of eating *Galletas Marias* in Mexico is to spread *cajeta*, a goat's-milk caramel spread (see page 212), on a cracker and top it with another one to make a sandwich; this was the usual dessert in my lunchbox. They can be used in layered desserts as you would use ladyfingers.

DATE AND VANILLA CRÈME BRÛLÉE

2 cups heavy cream

½ cup (packed) chopped dried pitted Medjool dates (about 5 ounces; see Tip)

1 vanilla bean, split in half lengthwise

5 large egg yolks

½ cup plus 4 tablespoons sugar

Dates were always around the house for snacking when I was a kid. Now I absolutely love to use them in both sweet and savory dishes. Large, dark-skinned Medjool dates are grown in the United States, Jordan, Israel, and now in Baja! I think they add a whole new dimension to an otherwise classic crème brûlée.

Preheat the oven to 350°F. Arrange four 1-cup ramekins inside a baking dish.

Combine the cream with the dates in a medium-size heavy saucepan. Scrape the seeds from the vanilla bean into the pan; add the bean too. Bring the cream mixture to a boil over medium-high heat. Reduce the heat and simmer for 5 minutes to blend the flavors.

Discard the vanilla bean and transfer the cream mixture to a blender. Blend for 5 minutes, or until very smooth.

Whisk the egg yolks and the ½ cup sugar in a medium bowl until the mixture is pale in color and very smooth. Gradually add the warm cream mixture to the yolks, whisking constantly.

Strain the mixture into a large measuring cup, and then pour it into the ramekins, dividing it equally. Add enough water to the baking dish to reach three quarters of the way up the sides of the dish. Carefully transfer the dish to the oven and bake for 45 minutes, or until the edges of the custards are set but the centers still jiggle slightly when the ramekins are tapped.

Remove the baking dish from the oven, and transfer the ramekins to a wire rack. Let the custards cool completely; then cover with plastic wrap and refrigerate them overnight.

Preheat the broiler.

Sprinkle 1 tablespoon sugar evenly over each custard. Place the ramekins on a small baking sheet and broil for 2 minutes, or until the sugar just starts to caramelize. (Alternatively, you can use a kitchen torch if you have one.) Refrigerate the custards for about 30 minutes, or until the tops harden, and then serve.

TIP DATES ARE MOST PREVALENT AT SUMMER'S END, WHEN DIFFERENT VARIETIES FROM BOTH CALIFORNIA AND THE MIDDLE EAST START SHOWING UP IN MARKETS, BUT THEY ARE WIDELY AVAILABLE YEAR-ROUND. WHILE THE MEDJOOL DATE IS CONSIDERED THE PREMIER VARIETY, ALL DATES HAVE VERY SIMILAR SUGAR CONTENT AND CAN BE USED IN THIS RECIPE. LOOK FOR SMOOTH AND SHINY FRUIT AND AVOID ANY THAT ARE SHRIVELED OR HAVE SUGAR CRYSTALS ON THE SURFACE. IF SUGAR CRYSTALS FORM AFTER YOU HAVE PURCHASED THEM, YOU CAN STEAM THE DATES FOR A FEW MINUTES TO ELIMINATE THEM. STORED IN THE FRIDGE, DATES CAN LAST UP TO ONE YEAR.

PASTEL DE TRES LECHES

Unsalted butter, for the pan

1½ cups all-purpose flour, plus more for the pan

1 tablespoon baking powder

1 teaspoon ground cinnamon

4 large eggs, separated

1½ cups sugar

½ cup whole milk

One 14-ounce can sweetened condensed milk

One 12-ounce can evaporated milk

1 cup heavy cream

2 tablespoons orange liqueur, such as Grand Marnier

Italian Meringue (recipe follows; optional)

This is a decadent and classic Mexican cake that you have to make at least once in your life (and if you do, I guarantee you'll make it again). A firm-textured cake, it holds up to being soaked in three kinds of milk/cream (hence the name *tres leches*). Traditionally it's topped with sweetened beaten raw egg whites, which could be dangerous for small kids and pregnant women, two groups that really enjoy this cake. An Italian meringue, which is made of cooked egg whites, is the perfect solution.

Preheat the oven to 350°F. Butter and flour a 10-inch cake pan with 2-inch-high sides, and then line the bottom with parchment paper. Butter the paper.

Mix the flour, baking powder, and cinnamon in a medium bowl.

Using an electric mixer, whip the egg whites until frothy. With the mixer running, gradually add the sugar and beat until stiff peaks form. Beat in the egg yolks, one at a time, blending well after each addition. Add the flour mixture in three additions, alternating with the whole milk in two additions.

Pour the batter into the prepared pan and bake for 30 minutes, or until a tester inserted into the center comes out clean. Let the cake cool slightly in the pan; then invert it onto a platter with 1-inch-high sides.

Pierce the top of the warm cake all over with a thick skewer. Mix the sweetened condensed milk, evaporated milk, heavy cream, and orange liqueur, and pour over the cake. Cover and refrigerate until cold, about 3 hours, or overnight.

Serve as is or frost the top with Italian meringue, if desired.

italian meringue

3 large egg whites, at room temperature

½ cup sugar

⅛ teaspoon cream of tartar

Italian meringue is a firm cooked meringue made with boiling sugar syrup. It can be used alone as a frosting, or I sometimes pipe it into rosettes and dry them out in a low oven for tasty treats. Use a candy thermometer to make sure the sugar syrup reaches 235°F. By adding the hot syrup to the egg whites while whipping, you'll be cooking them to approximately 140°F, the pasteurization temperature for eggs.

Put the egg whites in the bowl of an electric mixer, and set the mixer on low speed (you want to whip the whites just until foamy).

While the whites are slowly whipping, swirl ⅓ cup water and the sugar in a medium-size heavy saucepan over low heat until the sugar dissolves. Then raise the heat to medium-high and boil without stirring until the mixture registers 235°F on a candy thermometer and is the texture of corn syrup. Remove the pan from the heat.

Once the egg whites are foamy, add the cream of tartar to them and beat until soft peaks form. With the mixer running, add the hot syrup in a slow, steady stream. Beat until the whites are stiff and glossy and cool to the touch.

Use the meringue immediately.

COCADA
EASY COCONUT BARK

Nonstick cooking spray

5½ cups sweetened shredded coconut (one 14-ounce package)

½ cup sweetened condensed milk

These traditional baked coconut squares are served by street vendors all over Mexico. They take no time at all to prepare and are great for picnics and for packing in lunch boxes—if they last long enough! My favorite part of this dessert is the crunchy golden edges. When I make it at home, they disappear first.

Preheat the oven to 350°F. Spray a 13 x 9-inch glass baking dish with nonstick cooking spray.

Mix the coconut and condensed milk in a bowl until well blended. Spread the mixture out in the prepared baking dish and bake for 20 minutes, or until the coconut is evenly browned and dark and crisp at the edges. Cool slightly, and then cut into squares. Serve warm or at room temperature.

MESSY CAJETA WHIPPED CREAM NAPOLEON

Nonstick cooking spray

All-purpose flour, for rolling

1 frozen puff pastry sheet (half of a 17.3-ounce package), thawed

1 cup heavy cream

¼ cup *cajeta, dulce de leche,* or thick caramel sauce

¼ cup powdered sugar, plus more for sprinkling

Assortment of fresh berries, for garnish

The fact is, I could come up with a hundred different *cajeta* recipes. *Cajeta,* a caramel-like spread traditionally made with goat's milk, is readily available all over Mexico and is known as *dulce de leche* in other parts of Latin America. *Cajeta,* which translates as "small box," used to refer to the box in which the *cajeta* was sold. Now you can find it in a glass jar, a much more convenient presentation. It is found in many supermarkets and Latin markets and is available in different flavors, the most common being wine and strawberry. Any flavored *cajeta* would work well in this recipe. Whipped with cream and a little sugar, it is a perfectly sweetened filling for this tasty treat—which is just as delightful as it is messy to eat.

Preheat the oven to 400°F. Spray a large baking sheet with nonstick cooking spray.

Sprinkle a flat surface and a rolling pin with flour. Roll out the puff pastry sheet to ⅛-inch thickness. Cut it into three 13 x 4-inch rectangles. Sprinkle one of the rectangles generously with flour; then fold it, wrap it loosely in plastic wrap, and transfer it to the refrigerator.

Place the 2 remaining puff pastry rectangles on the prepared baking sheet. Spray the underside of a second baking sheet with nonstick cooking spray, and set it on top of the puff pastry rectangles (this is to prevent the puff pastry from rising). Bake for 12 minutes, or until the puff pastry is golden. Let the puff pastry cool completely. Repeat with the remaining puff pastry

RECIPE CONTINUES

rectangle, unfolding the dough and brushing off the flour and making sure the baking sheets are cool before using them. (The puff pastry can be prepared 1 day ahead. Wrap it tightly in plastic wrap and store at room temperature.)

Using an electric mixer, whip the cream, *cajeta,* and powdered sugar in a bowl to form stiff peaks. (The *cajeta* whipped cream can be made 1 day ahead. Cover and keep refrigerated.)

Cut each pastry rectangle into 4 squares. Place 1 puff pastry square on a plate. Top it with ¼ cup of the *cajeta* whipped cream. Top with a second puff pastry square, then ¼ cup *cajeta* whipped cream. Top with a third puff pastry square, and sprinkle it generously with powdered sugar. Repeat with the remaining puff pastry squares and *cajeta* whipped cream to make 4 napoleons. Garnish with fresh berries, and serve.

ARROZ CON LECHE
MEXICAN RICE PUDDING

1 cup long-grain
white rice

One 3-inch-long
cinnamon stick

¼ teaspoon salt

4 cups whole milk

1 cup sugar

5 large egg yolks

½ teaspoon vanilla extract

¾ cup raisins

There's a song I sang as a child with the words: *"Arroz con leche, me quiero casar con una senorita que sepa planchar,"* which means: "Rice pudding, I want to marry a lady who knows how to iron." I do not know how to iron, but I think my Mexican rice pudding more than compensates for my lack of certain domestic skills. You've got three delectable choices here: Serve this warm, as is done traditionally; serve it cold; or, once it is cold, churn it in an ice cream maker for a scrumptious ice cream, scooped and served on a sugar cone.

Place the rice in a bowl and add hot water to cover. Let stand at room temperature for 15 minutes. Then drain the rice, discarding the soaking liquid.

Combine 2 cups water with the rice, cinnamon stick, and salt in a medium-size heavy saucepan set over medium-high heat. Bring to a boil; then reduce the heat to low, and cover the pan. Simmer for 18 minutes, or until the mixture is dry. Add the milk and sugar and cook over low heat for 30 minutes, or until the mixture begins to thicken.

Whisk together the egg yolks and vanilla in a small bowl. Carefully remove ½ cup of the hot liquid from the rice mixture and whisk it into the egg yolk mixture. Whisk the egg yolk mixture back into the rice in the pan. Cook, stirring with a wooden spoon, over low heat for 3 minutes, or until the mixture coats the back of the spoon. Do not boil. Stir in the raisins. Cool the mixture slightly. Serve warm, or cover and refrigerate overnight and serve chilled.

FRESH GUAVA LAYER CAKE

CAKE LAYERS

Nonstick cooking spray

3 cups cake flour

1½ teaspoons baking powder

½ teaspoon salt

6 large eggs

2 teaspoons vanilla extract

1½ cups (3 sticks) unsalted butter, at room temperature

2½ cups granulated sugar

⅔ cup buttermilk

GUAVA FILLING

2 pounds fresh ripe guavas (each about the size of a golf ball), brown tops removed

1¼ cups granulated sugar

4 ounces cream cheese

Not only is this giant layer cake a stunner, it is absolutely delicious with its creamy guava filling and fluffy buttercream frosting. We had a guava tree in my mom's garden, and when the fruit was in season, we ate our share of guava cakes, guava tarts, guava water, and pretty much guava anything. This is my homage to my mom's guava tree.

To make the cake layers, position one rack in the top third and another rack in the bottom third of the oven, and preheat the oven to 325°F. Lightly spray three 9-inch nonstick cake pans with nonstick cooking spray.

Sift the flour, baking powder, and salt into a large bowl. Whisk the eggs and vanilla together in another bowl. Using an electric mixer, beat the butter in a large bowl until fluffy. Gradually add the granulated sugar, beating until well blended. Add the egg mixture in three additions, beating until well blended after each addition. Then beat in the flour mixture in three additions alternately with the buttermilk, scraping down the inside of the bowl occasionally.

Divide the batter among the prepared cake pans. Bake for 40 minutes, or until the layers are puffed and a tester inserted into the centers comes out clean. Transfer to wire racks and let the cake layers cool completely in the pans. Invert the cakes onto the racks. (The cake layers can be prepared 1 day ahead. Cover tightly with plastic wrap and store at room temperature.)

To make the guava filling, combine the guavas, ¾ cup water, and the granulated sugar in a medium-size heavy saucepan set over medium heat. Cover and bring to a boil. Then reduce the

CREAM CHEESE FROSTING

Three 8-ounce packages cream cheese, at room temperature

6 tablespoons (¾ stick) unsalted butter, at room temperature

1½ teaspoons vanilla extract

2¼ cups powdered sugar

2 cups chopped unsalted pistachios

heat to low and simmer, covered, for 5 minutes, or until the guavas begin to break and are tender. Drain the guavas, reserving the syrup. Cool both separately.

Seed and coarsely chop half of the guavas (they may fall apart slightly). Set the chopped guavas aside. Put the seeds in a blender and add the remaining guavas, the cream cheese, and 1 cup of the reserved syrup. Blend until the mixture is smooth. Strain the mixture into a large bowl, whisking the mixture in the strainer to extract as much of the liquid as possible. (Discard the solids.) Gently mix in the chopped guavas.

Place 1 cake layer, flat side up, on a platter. Brush 3 tablespoons of the remaining reserved syrup over the cake. Spread half of the guava filling over the top. Top with a second cake layer, brush with 3 tablespoons syrup, and spread with the remaining guava filling. Top with the third cake layer. Refrigerate until ready to frost. (Reserve the remaining syrup for another use; see page 218.)

To make the cream cheese frosting, use an electric mixer to beat the cream cheese, butter, and vanilla together until light and fluffy. Gradually beat in the powdered sugar. Cover and refrigerate for 25 minutes, or until firm enough to spread.

Spread the frosting over the top and sides of the cake. Coat the sides of the cake with the pistachios. (The cake can be prepared 2 days ahead. Cover and refrigerate.)

Cut into slices, and serve.

GUAVA SUGAR SYRUP

By no means discard the guava sugar syrup that you have left over after making the cake on page 217. It will keep in the refrigerator for weeks and can be used anywhere simple syrup is used, from soaking cakes (as it is used in this recipe) to cooking fruit to adding to frostings or sweetening drinks. Try sweetening freshly squeezed lime juice with the syrup for a refreshing guava lemonade, or pour a little into a martini shaker with some rum and strawberry puree for a Latin strawberry daiquiri. Or if you want to get really adventurous, cook it all the way down to a caramel color and add a little heavy cream for a guava-scented caramel!

MEXICAN CHOCOLATE SOUFFLÉ

1 tablespoon unsalted butter, melted

Four 3.1-ounce disks Ibarra chocolate (see page 117), coarsely chopped

6 tablespoons (¾ stick) unsalted butter

6 large egg yolks

6 large egg whites

¼ cup sugar

As we well know, chocolate has been around for a very long time, dating all the way back to pre-Columbian Mexico. Once considered a gift from the gods by the Mayans, and after being introduced to Europe, reserved for Spanish royalty, chocolate has become a worldwide favorite when preparing desserts. You'll find it in cakes, tarts, dessert sauces, and soufflés, as you see here. Mexican chocolate, available in Latin markets and some supermarkets, is flavored with cinnamon, almonds, and vanilla. It makes for an unmistakable—and irresistible—soufflé.

Preheat the oven to 400°F. Brush eight ½-cup ramekins or custard cups with the melted butter.

Set a large metal bowl over a saucepan of simmering water, add the chocolate and the 6 tablespoons butter to the bowl, and stir until the mixture is melted and smooth (the mixture will be a little grainy). Remove the bowl from the heat and let the mixture cool slightly. Then whisk in the egg yolks.

Using an electric mixer, whip the egg whites in a medium bowl until foamy. Add the sugar and beat until stiff peaks form. Fold the whites into the chocolate mixture in three additions. Divide the chocolate batter among the prepared ramekins.

Bake the soufflés for 16 to 18 minutes, or until they are puffed but the centers still jiggle slightly. Serve immediately.

APRICOT TEQUILA ICE CREAM

6 ounces dried pitted apricots, diced (1½ cups)

⅓ cup golden tequila

1 vanilla bean, split in half lengthwise

3 cups heavy cream

6 large egg yolks

6 tablespoons sugar

Tequila makes a tangy partner for sweet apricots in this fresh take on ice cream. Although nothing compares to the flavor and texture of ice cream made from scratch, you can take a shortcut and simply fold the tequila-soaked apricots into a half gallon of softened vanilla-bean ice cream from your supermarket.

Combine the apricots, tequila, and vanilla bean in a small jar. Cover, and let macerate overnight at room temperature.

The next day, set up an ice bath: Place a medium bowl in a large bowl of ice. Set a fine-mesh sieve over the medium bowl.

Remove the vanilla bean from the jar and put it in a medium-size heavy saucepan. (Set the tequila-soaked apricots aside.) Add the cream to the pan and bring to a boil over medium-high heat. While the cream is heating, whisk the egg yolks and sugar in a medium bowl until the mixture is pale in color and very smooth.

Gradually add the hot cream to the yolks, whisking constantly (discard the vanilla bean). Return the mixture to the saucepan and cook over low heat, stirring constantly with a wooden spoon, for about 4 minutes, until the custard registers 170° to 175°F on an instant-read thermometer and coats the back of the spoon.

Immediately pour the custard through the sieve into the bowl set in the ice bath. Let the custard cool, whisking it occasionally. Cover and refrigerate for 4 hours, until very cold, or overnight.

Pulse the apricots with the tequila in a food processor until they form a thick, chunky puree. Add ½ cup of the chilled custard and pulse to combine. Then stir the entire apricot mixture into the remaining custard. Churn the custard in an ice cream maker according to the manufacturer's instructions. Transfer the ice cream to an airtight container and freeze for 12 hours, or until hard.

TIP THERE'S NO DOUBT ABOUT IT, TEQUILA IS THE BEST CONTRIBUTION MEXICO HAS MADE TO THE WORLD! WE ARE DEFINITELY TEQUILA DRINKERS IN MY FAMILY. MY BROTHER GOES FOR THE *BLANCO*, OR SILVER, THE STRONGEST IN AGAVE FLAVOR SINCE IT'S BOTTLED IMMEDIATELY AFTER THE DISTILLATION PROCESS. MY DAD GOES FOR THE *REPOSADO*, OR RESTED, WHICH IS AGED FOR MORE THAN TWO MONTHS AND GENTLER ON THE PALATE. ORANGES ARE MANDATORY WITH HIS TEQUILA, AS BITING INTO A SWEET ORANGE WEDGE BALANCES AND FURTHER ENHANCES THE DRINK'S FLAVOR. I FAVOR *AÑEJOS*, OR AGED TEQUILAS, AND OFTEN PAIR THEM WITH *SANGRITA*, A SWEET-AND-SOUR TOMATO-BASED DRINK THAT IS SIPPED ALTERNATELY WITH THE TEQUILA. *ORO*, OR GOLDEN TEQUILA, IS PREFERRED FOR MAKING MIXED DRINKS, COOKING, AND BAKING; IT IS COMMONLY BLENDED WITH CARAMEL COLOR AND SUGAR SYRUP, SO IT TENDS TO BE SWEETER.

POMEGRANATE PINE NUT BRITTLE

Nonstick cooking spray

½ cup pure pomegranate juice

¼ cup sugar

¼ cup light corn syrup

4 tablespoons (½ stick) unsalted butter

1½ cups pine nuts, toasted

½ teaspoon salt

½ teaspoon baking soda

Using pomegranate juice instead of water to make this nut brittle not only makes for a beautiful magenta-tinted caramel color but also adds a very subtle flavor of the pomegranate. Serve this buttery treat with ice cream, or pack it in cellophane bags and tie them with festive bows for delicious party favors.

Grease a large baking sheet with nonstick cooking spray.

Combine the pomegranate juice, sugar, corn syrup, and butter in a medium-size heavy saucepan. Cook over medium heat, swirling the pan occasionally, for about 12 minutes, or until the mixture registers 305°F on an instant-read thermometer and is caramel in color. Remove the pan from the heat and immediately (and very carefully) whisk in the pine nuts, salt, and baking soda. Pour the mixture onto the prepared baking sheet (the mixture will spread out on its own). Allow the brittle to cool completely; then break into pieces and enjoy. The brittle will keep for several days in an airtight tin if you live in an area with low humidity.

CALABAZA WITH BROWN SUGAR

3 cups (packed) dark brown sugar

Two 3-inch-long cinnamon sticks

One 4-pound butternut squash, cut into 4-inch pieces (with peel and seeds)

Gloria Linss, grandmother of my editorial assistant, Valeria, was kind enough to provide us with the perfect ratio of sugar and cinnamon to squash for this recipe. She also pointed out that at her house they did not chop the squash; she would literally smash the whole gourd onto the kitchen floor until it broke into pieces. You can keep it old-school and do that, but I suggest you go with a very sharp knife: it makes cleanup easier. For a sweet finish, do as Gloria does and drizzle the squash with chilled evaporated milk before serving. The cold milk is the perfect counterpoint to the extravagantly sweet, melt-in-your-mouth cinnamon-scented squash.

Stir 6 cups water, the brown sugar, and the cinnamon sticks in a large heavy pot until the sugar dissolves. Add the squash and bring to a boil over high heat. Reduce the heat and simmer, uncovered, for 2½ hours, or until almost all of the liquid has evaporated, the mixture has thickened, and the squash is very tender. Remove the cinnamon sticks, let the squash cool slightly, and serve warm or at room temperature.

CHOCOFLAN

CARAMEL

1 cup granulated sugar

CHOCOLATE CAKE

½ cup boiling water

½ cup unsweetened cocoa powder

⅓ cup whole milk

1 teaspoon vanilla extract

1⅓ cups all-purpose flour

1 teaspoon baking soda

½ teaspoon salt

12 tablespoons (1½ sticks) unsalted butter, at room temperature, plus more for the pan

1 cup (packed) dark brown sugar

½ cup granulated sugar

3 large eggs

Made in a Bundt cake pan, this half flan, half chocolate cake is a decadent marriage of two dessert classics. The batter for the chocolate cake is made first, then poured into the Bundt pan, followed by the flan batter. The batters may appear to mix but they completely separate while baking, with the flan ending up on the bottom. I like to eat the cake warm, but traditionally it is chilled for 24 hours before serving.

Preheat the oven to 400°F. Butter a 10-inch nonstick Bundt pan (12-cup capacity).

To make the caramel, stir together the granulated sugar and ¼ cup water in a large heavy saucepan set over medium-high heat. Cook, brushing down the sides of the pan with a wet pastry brush to prevent crystals from forming, until the sugar melts and the mixture becomes a dark amber caramel. Working quickly and carefully, immediately pour the hot caramel into the prepared Bundt pan, tilting it to cover the bottom and halfway up the sides of the pan. Let the caramel cool completely for 4 hours or overnight in the refrigerator.

Place the caramel-coated Bundt pan in a roasting pan, and fill the roasting pan halfway with water.

To make the chocolate cake, whisk the boiling water and the cocoa powder in a medium bowl to blend. Whisk in the milk and the vanilla extract. In another medium bowl, whisk the flour, baking soda, and salt together.

RECIPE CONTINUES

FLAN

½ **cup evaporated milk**

½ **cup sweetened condensed milk**

2 **large eggs**

½ **teaspoon vanilla extract**

Using an electric mixer, beat together the butter, brown sugar, and granulated sugar until the mixture is pale and fluffy. Add the eggs, one at a time, beating well after each addition. Mix in the flour and cocoa mixtures alternately in batches, beginning and ending with the flour (the batter may separate; do not worry). Pour the batter into the Bundt pan.

To make the flan, combine the evaporated milk, condensed milk, eggs, and vanilla in a blender. Blend for 30 seconds on high speed, until smooth. Pour the mixture gently over the chocolate batter in the Bundt pan. Cover the pan with foil, and carefully transfer it, in the water-filled roasting pan, to the oven. Bake for 15 minutes.

Reduce the oven temperature to 350°F, and continue baking until a tester inserted into the cake comes out clean, about 1 hour.

Let the cake cool in the pan for 15 minutes. Then carefully run a small knife around the edge of the cake, and invert the cake onto a platter. Cool for 1 hour. Cover, and refrigerate overnight. Serve chilled.

TAMARIND MARTINIS

12 ounces shelled fresh
tamarind pods, rinsed
with cold water

1 cup sugar

¼ cup Mexican chile-lime
powder (see page 231)

1 lime wedge

6 salted plums

2 to 2½ cups vodka

There's no beating fresh tamarind pods (as opposed to the pulp)
for making the tamarind water for this recipe. Fresh tamarind
should look a little moist (and be sure to buy unsweetened
tamarind—sometimes it is sold coated with sugar to be eaten like
candy). Salted plums can be found in Mexican and Asian markets.
Mexican chile-lime powder will be in the candy aisle of the Mexican
market. Note that this is *not* chile powder or American chili powder.
It's meant to be eaten on its own or sprinkled on fresh fruit. If you
can't find the plums or the powder, just omit them both and mix
some sugar and salt together for the rim. For the teetotalers in the
house, including babies and moms-to-be, tamarind water is also
delicious on its own.

Combine the tamarind and 4 cups water in a medium-size
heavy saucepan set over medium-high heat, and bring to a
boil. Boil, uncovered, until the tamarind is very soft, 10 to
15 minutes.

Carefully pour the water into a container and set it aside.
Using a potato masher, mash the tamarind in the saucepan
(the seeds are still in there). Return the reserved tamarind
water to the saucepan and mix it into the mashed pulp. Then
strain the mixture into a pitcher, pressing on the solids to
extract as much liquid as possible. (Discard the solids.) Stir in
3 cups fresh water (the mixture should be fairly concentrated).
Add the sugar and stir until it is dissolved. (The tamarind water
can be made 2 days ahead and refrigerated.)

RECIPE CONTINUES

Put the chile-lime powder on a small plate. Using the lime wedge, moisten the rims of 6 martini glasses. Invert the martini glasses into the powder on the plate to coat the rims. Turn the glasses right side up and put 1 salted plum in each glass. Set aside.

For each serving, combine ¾ cup tamarind water and ¼ cup vodka in a cocktail shaker with ice. Shake vigorously. Strain into a prepared martini glass and serve. (Alternatively, you can mix all the tamarind water, all the vodka, and some ice in a large pitcher and just pour the mixture into each martini glass for a faster preparation.)

MICHELADA PREPARADA

1 cup clam-tomato juice (preferably Clamato)

5 tablespoons fresh lime juice

½ cup plus 2 teaspoons Mexican chile-lime powder (see page 231)

1 teaspoon bottled hot sauce (such as Tabasco sauce)

1 teaspoon Worcestershire sauce

1 teaspoon Maggi seasoning sauce (see page 28)

1 lime wedge

4 bottles Mexican beer, ice-cold

Micheladas are my drink of choice. It's a simple beverage: a little fresh lime juice and salt mixed with an ice-cold beer in an ice-filled mug. This recipe is for the *Michelada Preparada,* also known as the *Michelada Cubana* where I grew up, a spicy and tangy version made with a clam-tomato juice. I decided to freeze the mixture into cubes so I can always have them available for myself or unexpected company. Pucker up and beware, unless you're Mexican! The ice cubes are supposed to melt slightly into your beer for a refreshing and zesty drink that is thought to cure even the worst hangover.

Mix the clam-tomato juice, lime juice, 2 teaspoons chile-lime powder, the hot sauce, Worcestershire sauce, and Maggi sauce in a small bowl to combine. Pour the mixture into an ice cube tray (any shape ice cube will work) and freeze.

Chill 4 beer mugs until very cold.

Put the ½ cup chile-lime powder on a small plate. Wet the rim of each beer mug with the lime wedge. Invert the mugs onto the chile-lime powder to coat the rims. Put the mugs right side up and place 2 or 3 *Michelada* ice cubes in each mug. Pour the beer over the ice cubes, sprinkle with a little of the chile-lime powder, and serve.

GLOSSARY

Fresh Chiles

ANAHEIM CHILE: Named after the city in California, this generally mild chile is one of the most commonly available in the United States; it is usually medium green in color and has a long narrow shape. When dried, it is referred to as a California chile.

ÁRBOL CHILE: A small thin green chile, full of seeds. It has a quick sharp heat. When dried, árbol chiles turn red in color.

GÜERO CHILE: Most chiles in Mexico that are light yellow or very pale green are called güero chiles. They are very mild in flavor and are great for stuffing and frying.

HABANERO CHILE: Small, round with ridges, orange-gold in color. These are always extremely hot and should be handled and eaten with caution. Habaneros are most flavorful when *asado* (seared in a pan) and are never skinned. Uncooked, they are perfect for pickling and in fresh salsas.

JALAPEÑO CHILE: A rounded, dark green, shiny chile, 3 to 4 inches in length. It is pleasantly hot and fresh-tasting. Used (raw) in salsas, charred, pickled, sliced into rings, and stuffed. When ripened on the plant, they turn red in color. Chipotles are smoke-dried jalapeños.

POBLANO CHILE: A widely used fresh chile; dark green, large, and wide, with shiny skin. It is used in many traditional Mexican dishes such as *rajas* (see page 188) and chiles relleno (stuffed, battered, and fried poblanos). Ripened on the plant and dried, it is known as chile ancho or pasilla.

SERRANO CHILE: The preferred chile for salsas. Slender, bullet-shaped, 2 to 3 inches long. Used raw or charred in salsas. Usually hotter than jalapeños, these range between hot and very hot.

Dried Chiles

ANCHO CHILE (also known as pasilla): A broad chile, 3 to 4 inches long. The flavor ranges from mild to pungent. The rich, slightly fruit-flavored ancho is the sweetest of the dried chiles. The chile should be flexible and not too dried out. In its fresh green state, the ancho is called a poblano chile.

CASCABEL CHILE: A plum-shaped, dark-blood-red chile that ranges in size from about 1 to 1½ inches in diameter. *Cascabel* means "little round bell" or "rattle" in Spanish, a name alluding to the rattling sound this chile makes when shaken. It is commonly used in salsas to add a rich nutty flavor and mild heat.

CHIPOTLE CHILE: This hot chile is a smoked-dried jalapeño. It has a wrinkled dark brown skin and a smoky, sweet, almost chocolaty flavor. By far, my favorite chile for cooking.

GUAJILLO CHILE: The chile most commonly used in red salsas and enchiladas. Dark red to almost black, shiny, 6 to 8 inches in length. Because of their thick flesh, guajillos need to be soaked or fully cooked before using for salsas.

MORILLA CHILE: Also known in Baja as the *mora* chile, this is a smaller jalapeño that is smoke-dried until it is the color of a mulberry (*mora*), hence its name. It's a narrow chile about 2½ inches long and ¾ inch wide. The flavor is similar to that of the chipotle, which is a good substitute.

MULATO CHILE: A different variety of dried poblano that looks very similar to the ancho (the dried version of the poblano) but has a slightly sweeter flavor. When rehydrated it is perfect for stuffing and has a mild chocolate taste.

Cheese

AÑEJO OR COTIJA CHEESE: A type of salty, crumbly cow's-milk cheese that is considered the Mexican feta. It is one of only a few cheeses in Mexico with a strong pungent, salty flavor. It is available in Latin markets and some supermarkets.

COTIJA CHEESE: See Añejo cheese.

EMMENTHAL: Switzerland's oldest and most important cheese, named for the country's Emmenthal Valley. It has a mellow, buttery, nutty flavor that is suitable in sauces and as a grated topping.

FRESCO CHEESE: A salty, rubbery, wet cheese. It crumbles easily, like a cow's-milk feta. It is commonly used to sprinkle over finished dishes such as tostadas, taquitos, and enchiladas.

MANCHEGO CHEESE: An aged Spanish sheep's-milk cheese, very popular in Mexico.

OAXACA CHEESE: A creamy cheese with a delicate flavor; it melts at a low temperature and has a tendency to run and string. It is used in quesadillas or simply fried and eaten with tortillas. A dry mozzarella works as a substitute.

PANELA CHEESE: Easy to identify by the distinctive woven pattern pressed into the outside by the basket used for molding. Its flavor is mild and sweet. It is commonly used for snacking on its own and is very popular because it is low in fat. Make sure to ask for panela *cheese* when looking for this ingredient; in Mexico, the raw sugar cones, known as *piloncillo,* are also called *panela.*

GRACIAS

I grew up with a father who constantly told my brother, Antonio, my sister, Carina, and me, *"No hay pecado mas grande que el de ser ingrato"* ("There is no greater sin than that of being ungrateful"). Even though I've got my mom up there pulling some strings, I'll be sure to include everyone who's helped me along the way, just in case my dad is right.

I was very much mistaken when I thought my mom, Lucha, wasn't going to see me write my first book, as she has been with me every step of the way. Thank you, Mom, for a love so powerful that it is just as strong now that you're gone as it was when you were still here.

Dad (a.k.a. Tony Bolloni), every day I'm getting closer to getting you that Harley. It's not just my passion for spreading the word about Mexican food that motivates me; it's that bike with a big red bow. Thank you for the words of wisdom along the way: they are the extended hand that helps me get up every time I fall.

Cari, how lucky are we that someone decided that we not only get to be sisters but also get to be best friends? I thank God every day just for you. Toño, you don't even have to say anything and I know how much you love and support me. The size of your heart and the strength with which you carry it are what make you the amazing person you are. Thank you both for your belief in me.

To my beloved son, Fausto Antonio Gallardo Valladolid, alias *"el guapo,"* none of this means anything without you. Everything I will ever do will always be for you. How is it that such a tiny human could change my life, give me purpose and perspective, and help me finally understand the depth of the love my parents had for me? Don't know how, don't care how. I just enjoy every second of every day I have with you. Fausto (dad), thank you for my son and for your support. *Isa, Dani, Gaby, Luis To, y Pa. Mis bebes. Todos son mis bebes.*

To the best-looking family on earth (according to my aunt Martha), the Rodriguez clan: Tia Chela, Deme, Andres, Ernie, Raymundo, Lola, Christian, Denise, Pru, Coque, Moni, Tia Martha, Gorda, Guero, Feban, Euge, and Clau. Thank you for letting me be a part of the tightest family I know.

Tia Marcela, you inspired my culinary career *and* you let me steal your recipes. Elsa Flores and Andres Brambila, thanks for sharing your restaurant secrets.

Valeria "Chils" Linss, you've not only been the best assistant known to man, you've also become a great friend and confidante and my son's favorite aunt (after Carina, of course). You've got a bright future ahead of you, kid, and I'll be pushing you every step of the way.

Thanks to my best friend, Jos Matthews, and my favorite Peace Corps veteran, Amy Spindler, because sometimes I think (and write) in Spanish and you ladies make it make sense.

To the *"guapos"* and *"guapas"* at William Morris: Eric Lupfer, Lisa Grubka, Raul Mateu, Phillip Button, Albert Garcia, and Pedro Bonilla. Thank you for pulling me by the bathing suit strings and not letting me jump in the water until the coast was clear.

To Rica Allannic at Clarkson Potter, your perfect guidance made it both easy and fun to write this book. Amy Sly, thanks for your beautiful and sleek design. Amy Kalyn Sims, you made my vision come to life with your extraordinary skills as a photographer. Danielle Nowak, your faithful assistant, was a delight to work with. To Megan Schlow, my food stylist: it's an honor to hear you say that you'd actually like to purchase this cookbook! Alberto Machuca, just like magic (but with a little makeup) you miraculously knocked ten years off my face. Denise Canter, my prop stylist, you picked the perfect plate for every salsa.

To all my friends and loved ones, this is only the beginning. Life is so much sweeter (actually spicier) because every single one of you is in it. *Gracias amores, los quiero. Ciao!*

INDEX